# Life Fran

*By*

*V.G. Brooks*

# Table of Contents

# Acknowledgment and Dedication

Many have helped me on this journey. They are too numerous to name. So I won't. I dedicate this work to Bill, Sidney, Obie, and Jannie. I am sorry for not naming everybody, but you know who you are.

# Prologue

Mine is not necessarily a remarkable story. Like most of us, I started life as a child; I survived this condition, and I have spent the majority of my life getting over it. This is the story of my journey.

My first seventeen years were spent in a small western Kentucky town where the accident of birth landed me in the "integration generation." I went to college less than 50 miles away. I lived the civil rights movement, but it was the televised Watergate hearings that set my life mission—to work for a just society and for honest, responsive public institutions. That resolve led me to the nation's capital, Washington, D.C.—then called "Chocolate City"—where I met like-minded young people, especially a committed group of women of color. We were united in our determination to make a difference in our country and society. We leaned on each other to achieve this and to make our voices heard—not only by the federal government and its leaders but also by both the civil rights and women's rights movements. Self-righteous and somewhat arrogant, like most of the young, my sisters did do some good. In today's climate, it appears much of that good is being undone and maligned.

But I ramble. This is not a political book, except in the sense that I lived through a time of great change that shaped me as it did many others. This book tells my story against that backdrop. I was driven to write it because I see today women, people of color, people of different religions, and others all under attack and fighting the same fights that my friends and I fought some decades before. I am heartbroken by the hate and rage that is tacitly accepted by our leaders. But I am buoyed by the outpouring of activism that I see in our young people. I feel a kinship that spans generations.

The stories in this book are personal, but the experience of struggling, overcoming, and finding one's self is universal. Most people (including me) eventually arrive at some point of peace and resolve. If nothing else, we outlive our tormentors and have only to fight their lingering effects. Not that I speak lightly of these battles, mind you. Still, this is all my rather simplistic way of saying that we are born; we grow up; we live; and, along the way, we somehow manage to banish most if not all of our demons. If we are lucky, our existence has been of benefit to a person, family, community, country, or to the planet.

I offer this book to you, Dear Reader, with humility. There is no great profundity in its pages. It may offer some useful lessons and insights. Some will find parallels with things in their own lives. My salute to those who have "been there." I also hope that everyone will find several laughs. For me, the ironic, bittersweet, and funny experiences are the ones that really stuck, and that helped most to make me who I am today. I hope the message is one of resilience and the ability of even a wounded psyche to triumph. There are 17 vignettes, which can be enjoyed separately or read through from beginning to end. As you read each one, let it remind you of something in your life. Then, tell *your* story to a loved one—a partner, a child, a family member, a friend.

So, enjoy.

VG Brooks, February 2018

Warning: I don't know if this is a memoir in the strictest sense of the genre, but it certainly is memoir-like. I tried to pin down and confirm facts where I could, but this book relies mostly on my own faulty memory. Sometimes an event or experience just had no ending—or at least none I could recall—or sometimes there were gaps, and so I supplied my own fillers, trying to remain true to the feelings I had at the time. So be alerted: everything is true—except what isn't. But all of it is a genuine reflection of my life experience.

# 1: Wild Beginnings: My Country Idyll

I was born in a ramshackle farm house on the outskirts of Hopkinsville, a mid-sized city in western Kentucky. The house belonged to my maternal grandparents, Daddy Ernest and Big Hattie Gregory. Daddy Ernest worked at the local grain mill, and Big Hattie was a much-in-demand cook for rich white families. It was my grandmother's second marriage; before she married Daddy Ernest, she had been a Chilton. The older Chilton children were in constant conflict with the Gregory household. Ours was a three-generation household that consisted of my grandparents; their two youngest children, Margaret, my mother, and Fannie; and Fannie's daughter, Diane; and me. I don't know whether it was a happy household or not, but it was one in which I felt comfortable and loved. My father, Philip, was a frequent visitor. Later, Margaret's other loves came by—Edward, briefly a lover and a lifelong friend; and, AB (initials only), whom she later married.

My life was full, usually joyous, and I lived with abandon—from the moment I opened my eyes each morning until late at night when I was forced into sleep. While the adults worked, I was cared for by my nurse, Gwen, who lived next door. She took care of every need, and I was treated like an adjunct family member, eating her mother's good cooking and shadowing her father, Mr. Jack. Unlike children today, I was not over-scheduled, and I was able to explore the large yards, play with Geronimo, our dog, daydream, and play with my cousin. (Diane was cared for by Norma, Gwen's sister.) Diane and I were each other's given, each other's most important thing, and we had no need for other children. When my grandfather came home, he and I were inseparable, and I was often perched drowsing on his lap while he rocked in his hickory rocking chair. Even when his legs grew numb, he refused to relinquish my sleep-heavy body.

I was a keen observer and curious about everything. It took me a long time to decide to walk with or to talk to anyone besides Gwen and Daddy Ernest. But I was so alive in my mind. According to family lore, when I finally decided to communicate with the outside world, I took off like a veteran, speaking sentences from the start. The things that I said showed I had been listening all those months. No crawling or dragging along on the floor for me, either. I wobbled and stood on the first try—or so I'm told. A bit surprised at this new perspective on the world, I somehow started stepping out. It was shaky, but still . . . never an unsure step or a faltering. Not for a second directionless. (I was trying to catch up with Daddy Ernest—fearing that he had left me behind.) I staggered Frankenstein-like, lurching forward, hands conducting an air symphony. Slow, cold molasses-snail-sloth speed. But still, I moved forward, faster and surer that I'd catch him. I was over 40 before it dawned on me that Daddy Ernest had been purposely teasing me onward, tricking me into literally taking the next step in my development. Now I believe these first steps set me on my way to achieving what he always had wanted for his children: to see them stride out boldly into the world. Unafraid. Bursting with unending curiosity. Breathing in the world. Knowing that I was entitled to every beautiful and wondrous thing that the earth—indeed, the universe—had to offer. I graced the earth with each step. (Or at least that's my fantasy.)

When I was three, Aunt Fannie married Richard Simmons, a soldier and musician, and she and Diane moved to his hometown of St. Louis, Missouri. I was heartbroken. For a while, Uncle Richard drove Fannie and Diane down to see us on weekends. As they packed to return home, I'd sometimes get in the car and refuse to move. Uncle Richard often would intervene and get permission for me to go with them and return the following weekend. Those trips later morphed into summer vacations for Diane and me together, split between St. Louis and Hopkinsville. By then, I was riding the train by myself from Hopkinsville to St. Louis. (It was a different time.) I'd go to St. Louis alone, but Margaret would come up at the end of the summer and ride back home with me. In the city, surrounded by a bushel of new cousins and aunts and uncles, Diane quickly grew beyond me. (Being part of a rapidly expanding family just never took for

Aunt Fannie, who remained an outsider the rest of her life.)There were lots of diversions, and everyone in the city knew Uncle Richard. Diane also gained a larger audience, whose members could admire her new dresses and beauty. I was interested only in Diane. But it was during those summers that I watched Uncle Richard in his role as a family man—hard-working, soft-spoken, supportive. It was the first time I had experienced this sort of behavior, and for me, it set a standard for what a real man should be like. He was my ideal. He always called me "Miss Lorraine." He worked several jobs to support his family, but he was also a successful jazz musician, a champion bowler, and a son and spirit of St. Louis (since his days as a high school athlete). Despite his widespread popularity, he remained "old school," considering it his duty to not only provide but to shelter his family from the rampant racism in St. Louis and the surrounding areas. Even after death, he remains the most moral and selfless man I ever knew. He spawned many daydreams about my having a father like that in my own life. I fantasized that my dad was just like him. (My husband is a lot like him. Shortly after Bill and I married, my fondest wish came true: he and Uncle Richard met and liked each other, doubtlessly recognizing kindred spirits.) Despite my frequent stays in St. Louis, my wild-child life was centered in the big house on the outskirts of Hopkinsville.

In Hopkinsville, Daddy Ernest and Gwen created a world in which I mattered and in which I had power. Although Margaret (I never called her mother) was part of the household, she usually lived on the periphery of my universe. I, too, lived in this idyll for eight years. Although Daddy Ernest never complained, years of hard labor had taken a toll on his health, and he was failing. I don't know exactly what eventually killed him, but I do know that it was a wasting death. I think he was helped along by undiagnosed maladies, including diabetes, as well as a married life of vinegar and bile. Big Hattie was also ill, with the kinds of chronic, deadly illnesses that seemed always to plague Southern black women who ransomed their lives to rich white families. I didn't care much about her. She seemed to care even less about me and spoke about me usually just to complain about how light-skinned I was. She grew more and more ill, and she died with little fanfare or notice from me. Maybe it was just in my family, but in those days, children were kept ignorant of the fact and ritual of death. We were never at funerals. Certainly not at wakes. Many years later, I was surprised to learn that the traditions of some of my friends brought the fact, face, and body of death right into the house. They were not shut away like me, to emerge into a world in which the dead person's existence has been brutally excised as though he or she has never been. I remember the silence that slapped against my inevitable question—"Where's Big Hattie?" It did not take long for me to learn that important questions could not be asked aloud and that they could only be answered by own keen observation and study. Adults had no answers.

So I should not have been taken by surprise when it came to be my turn to disappear. It was Daddy Ernest who died, but I was the one who disappeared. I was eight years old. My day was typical. Times with Gwen and her family interspersed with me running in and out of the house. I remember it had been a long time since I sat on Daddy Ernest's lap, which was my favorite seat in the house. He said he was tired, but I didn't care. I was just happy being near him. More importantly, I knew he felt the same. But after supper one day, Margaret started putting all my clothes and toys and school books into boxes. She never said a word, and neither did anyone else. One of her male friends (I think it might have been AB; as I remember, he was on the scene at that point) came to the house and began loading the boxes into his car. Margaret threw a sweater around her shoulders (I remember it being green) and, with no good-byes to anyone, swept me out of the house and into the back seat of the car. I am stunned now that I said nothing. Until then, I had been an unafraid, outspoken, quick-to-question child. I don't know how long we drove. We stopped in front of a house illuminated by a big porch light. Margaret got me out of the car and nudged me along past the door being held open by a large and most handsome woman. (I didn't know the word "handsome" then, but I did know this woman seemed familiar.)

Margaret and the woman talked. AB stayed in the car until Margaret called to him. He began bringing the boxes into the house. The woman, who I was to know as Aunt Carrie, directed him to place the boxes in a small bedroom. I was sent there and instructed to unpack and put away my belongings. I did as I was told. I wasn't sure if I had figured out what was happening, but I did know that I would not be going back home—back to my Daddy Ernest. I just didn't know I'd never see him again. I didn't know that he would sicken greatly and die and be buried and mourned and that no one would even tell me. I only knew that when I crossed Aunt Carrie's doorstep, Daddy Ernest and Gwen disappeared from my life as I had from theirs. I ached so deep down; the pain was cellular. I closed my heart so that I wouldn't die. In only one night, with no spoken words, the wild was taken from me.

## 2: Little Bit

My great Aunt Carrie was a famous beauty who had dispatched two husbands under what locals referred to as "special" circumstances. Husband Number One, a retiree from the post office (one of the top jobs for a black man then), wanted a companion to rejoice in his fishing prowess and other wonderful attributes. Appropriately, he drowned in a boating accident while on a fishing trip with the man who would become Husband Number Two.

Husband Number Two was a drinker and lay-about who regularly berated my aunt and maybe even hit her on one occasion. His mishap involved a straight razor and defied the laws of physics, but apparently not those of the Hopkinsville police force. (Officially, he rolled over in his sleep onto a straight razor across the throat.) At the time of his demise, it was a community-wide secret that the sheriff was Aunt Carrie's long-time lover.

Uncle Herbert was my aunt's third and final husband. He counted himself lucky to have won her. I thought he should have been more thankful to have outlived her! Over six feet tall, he was caramel-colored all over, except for his closely-cropped grey-white hair, bushy grey eyebrows, and large staring grey eyes. His long extremities ended in shovel-sized hands and feet, and he walked with a just noticeable halt in his gait. Uncle Herbert was as kind as he was ignorant. He adored Aunt Carrie and all that was hers. That included me.

Aunt Carrie was Daddy Ernest's youngest sister. I first met Aunt Carrie and Uncle Herbert that night when I was eight years old, and my mother took me to live with them. We arrived at their home after dark. My things and I were shown to a room, where I was told to wait. From the adults' tones, I just knew my former life was over. I would live with Aunt Carrie and Uncle Herbert for seven years until Aunt Carrie's death. It was common in the black community to place children with relatives during times of crisis, and I now realize Margaret did this so she could devote her energies to caring for Daddy Ernest. But I didn't understand anything then, and nobody bothered to tell me. After about a year, I figured out that Daddy Ernest had died. Nobody told me; I never went to his funeral. In the meantime, Gwen (my nurse) went off to college and into a state job. I would not see her again until I was in my 50s. Although adults had decided that truth was not necessary for a child, it did not stop them from talking to each other in my presence as though somehow I was deaf to their words. As a "good" child, I was to speak when spoken to and not listen to "grown folks'" talk. How foolish! My ears were always attuned to adult voices and especially to how what they said never seemed to quite match how they acted or what they deemed appropriate to tell me. I never let on.

Just as adults did not explain their actions to me, I, in turn, never explained my thoughts to them. I knew *them* while they didn't know *me*, and that's the way I liked it. Later, as an adult, I recognized this as a survival tactic of oppressed and marginalized peoples everywhere—the response of the powerless to the powerful.

I only allowed myself a moment of regret on realizing I was to be separated from everyone and everything I loved. I worked determinedly to "disappear" that former life from my mind and heart. And I had the federal government to thank for this amazing ability. The year I was born, 1951, the Federal Civil Defense Administration produced the film "Duck and Cover," which was used up until the mid-1960s to terrorize school children about the specter of total annihilation. As young students, we learned, upon hearing the blast of the civil defense horn, to duck under our desks and cover our heads just like Bertie, the turtle star of the film, did whenever he encountered danger. For us, the danger was the threat of Soviet nuclear warheads vaporizing us and bombing mankind "back to the Stone Age." The gravity of the situation was drilled into us as we learned first aid and how to treat the few expected survivors of the nuclear holocaust for radiation burns and other fallout maladies. Each drill left me with the fear of walking out of school into a world populated by destroyed buildings, fried people, hordes fighting to break into well-stocked bomb shelters, and no way to reach anyone I loved. My survival response was to methodically work through the list of people closest to me and to "disappear" them mentally and emotionally from my life. This was no make-believe game. I mourned them hard and deeply until I came out the other end, knowing that I could survive without them. From the moment my bags and boxes were unpacked at Aunt Carrie's and Uncle Herbert's, I had already "disappeared" everyone and everything from my old life and turned my full attention to fitting in to this new life.

Their house was compact compared to my grandfather's large, drafty farmhouse with its big yards dotted with snowball bushes, fruit trees, a lush vegetable garden, and a pen for chickens. But here I had my own room, where adults knocked before entering. This was new and appealed to me. The room was neither too big nor too small; it was cozy, but there was enough room to hold the thoughts and feelings of a young girl and the first of a lifetime of journals.

Uncle Herbert got up early each morning, ate his standard breakfast of oatmeal while Aunt Carrie packed his lunch, and then went off to work at Western State, the "crazy" hospital on the edge of town. That good state-paid job afforded him plenty of time to "rest his eyes" while patients plied brooms and mops in his stead. At least one patient was always assigned the task of alerting Uncle Herbert whenever a supervisor was nearby. Sometimes, they forgot. (After all, they *were* crazy.) Supervisors often caught him in a relaxed pose with his eyes closed. They gave him verbal reprimands, but he never seemed at risk of being fired. He held this job until he retired.

During our settling-in period, Uncle Herbert took it upon himself to find me an appropriate nickname. (I recall him using my given name only twice in the five-plus years I lived with him and Aunt Carrie.) He finally settled on "Black Mammy." "Black Mammy," he'd say, "bring Uncle Herbert [pronounced "Hubbert"] a glass of ice water." (He always referred to himself in the third person. No reason.) He didn't sound angry when he said it, so I never figured out if he was being intentionally mean or if he was making a kind of opposite joke (we were both light-skinned). Maybe he was trying to prepare me for life in a newly desegregated world. His second favorite nickname was "Little Bit." Fortunately, this was the one he used when we were in public. But I answered to all. Names didn't matter. I knew who I was.

My own routine consisted of going to school, playing with neighborhood friends, and daydreaming about one day being "away." I wasn't too clear about where "away" was, but I knew it wasn't in Hopkinsville. Each Sunday, I attended Aunt Carrie's Freeman Chapel A.M.E. (African Methodist Episcopal) Church, where I was the pianist and, later, an usher. Aunt Carrie took it upon herself to teach me the sewing arts—knitting, crocheting, and quilting. I spent many hours working on quilts and other projects with Aunt Carrie and her women friends and listening to them "talk story" and make pronouncements. Even now, I miss the intimacy of this fellowship of women.

My most important pastime was watching Uncle Herbert. He just had his own special way of doing things and being in the world. One time, after slipping on a living room rug, he railed through the house, nailing down rugs and runners and anything that had the misfortune of being on the floor. People coming into the house were frequently baffled when they tripped on the unmoving edges of floor coverings. Another time, when he had been talked into escorting Aunt Carrie to one of her Eastern Star sorority affairs, he decided it was time to put an end to the foolishness of spending good money on rarely worn shoes. He dug up his old work brogans and slathered them with house paint, transforming them into the perfect dress shoes. Unfortunately, once they dried, the leather cracked, and a small shower of black paint flakes erupted with each step he took. Perhaps his most questionable act was his rush of sentimentality that brought a stray tomcat into the house. For some reason, the cat was dubbed Cousin Tommy. Cousin Tommy had a wound on his back, and to keep him from scratching it, Uncle Herbert tied up Cousin Tommy's right rear leg. Unfortunately, he tied it too tight, and the lower portion of the leg fell off. No matter: Tommy didn't seem to mind being a gimp. He was totally devoted to my aunt and uncle and each evening demanded his share of their nightly bottles of booze. Sated, he navigated the household each night on his three good feet and one bone: "tip, tip, tip, thunk." A weird syncopation that I grew used to.

Aunt Carrie and Uncle Herbert were inept, ineffective, and mutually destructive. They were also loving, God-fearing, decent people. Everyone who met them saw immediately that they were special. They granted me a precious and rare gift—the supreme compliment of being left alone to observe and think and create in my own mind. Living with them, I was allowed to direct my own life and to dwell in a dream world fueled by age-inappropriate literature like Colette and Henry Miller—all without adult interference.

Uncle Herbert's real passion was painting and wallpapering. For that job, he donned white bib overalls and carried a big, white carpenter's bag with "INTERIOR DECRATING" [decorating] stenciled in big black letters on the side. I sometimes got to escort him to and from jobs in the neighborhood, three of my skips to each of his long strides, awash in the greetings that a Southern stroll generated.

"Hello, Mr. Herbert."

"Hot today, Mr. Herbert."

Uncle Herbert never spoke or paused; he just gave a brief nod to each person.

The summer I was nine, I was given the special honor of being Uncle Herbert's official helper on a wallpapering job. After our parade through the neighborhood, we arrived at the house where the store already had delivered rolls of patterned paper, buckets, and the mix for making a paste. Uncle Herbert set to work methodically, measuring the walls, unrolling the wallpaper, and cutting the panels. I ran the water to mix the paste and stirred it to the right consistency.

"Um huh. That's about right, Little Bit," he'd say. I smiled at his praise.

A dip of the foot-wide brush, a broad sweep of paste onto the paper, and we were off! Uncle Herbert frowned in concentration as he carefully placed the paper panel against the wall. It was nice paper, with a kitchen motif that had to be lined up exactly. Once he was satisfied with the placement, he brought out a clean, dry brush and swept down the length of the panel, smoothing it onto the wall from top to bottom. (You had to be careful to smooth out all the bubbles and creases.) This action was repeated—measure, cut, paste, smoothe—until it was time for lunch, when we sat in companionable silence eating bologna sandwiches and drinking pop. When we finished, I always knew what would come next:

"Little Bit, it's time for Uncle Hubbert's nip."

This was the signal for me to put my shoes back on so I could go to the liquor store and pick up Uncle Herbert's "nip." A half-pint of Black & White scotch whiskey, distinguished by a photo of two schnauzers on the label. One black, one white. (In more than 50 years of drinking, I've never seen this particular stuff on a shelf.) I was eager to be outside.

Since I carried no money, I guess no one would, technically, be guilty of selling liquor to a minor. It was not even a concern. The police in our town were pragmatic and didn't enforce any laws that might prove inconvenient. Regardless, I was just anticipating the candy treat I usually got paid for this errand. The store was only a short distance away.

On entering the store, I minded my manners and spoke a general hello to the room. Some nodded in my direction, but a few turned away as though they were embarrassed for me to see them there. I went directly to the candy shelves and took a long time looking over each row of choices. I had been here often. The choices never changed. I always spent time recalling how each possible choice would taste. I picked up a Clark bar, mostly attracted to the orange wrapper. I got almost to the counter when I started thinking about all the other choices left behind. I returned the Clark bar and started over. After a second false start, I finally settled on a bag of

M&Ms (which would last all afternoon) and hurriedly placed my selection on the counter before I could change my mind.

"Hey, Little Bit, I see you're here for Uncle Herbert's mid-day nip. I've got it right here, all packaged up for you. You tell Mr. Herbert 'hello' for me, now." The counterman's face was friendly and familiar. I nodded and picked up the small brown sack.

The return trip was slower, and I enjoyed being with myself clothed in summer. Back at the work site, we took time for Uncle Herbert's nip and my candy. Soon, but maybe not so soon, we started back to work.

Powered by his lunchtime nip, Uncle Herbert no longer needed measuring sticks. With one quick glance, he was able to match the length and pattern of each wallpaper panel, pasting and smoothing, like someone running from the law. Somewhere along the way, we ran out of wall on one side of the kitchen, where a three-inch flap of paper hung over. Uncle Herbert was a professional, after all, and he quickly solved the problem—by pasting the overage onto the adjacent refrigerator.

"Uncle Herbert, that's the refrigerator."

"Yep. Yep. We'll cut around it later. Uncle Hubbert knows what he's doing."

I suppressed a giggle and settled down to watch what was beginning to look like one of those madcap scenes from "I Love Lucy." As the afternoon progressed, Uncle Herbert picked up his pace, letting neither counters nor appliances nor windows get in the way of wallpapering this room.

Soon it was quitting time.

"Uncle Herbert, aren't we going to finish the room?" There was one wall left. Luckily, it was the one with the door.

"This is a big job, Little Bit. We'll finish up tomorrow."

Uncle Herbert stood back and surveyed the day's accomplishment. Satisfied, he packed up his satchel for our walk home. On the way, we stopped by the liquor store, where he paid for his lunchtime nip and my candy and picked up his evening nip. The same liquor. The same half-pint. Perfectly sized for the back pocket of his overalls.

We set an agreeable pace going home, nodding and smiling to the greetings of neighbors who had come out on their porches to escape the indoor heat and see who was passing by.

"Hello, Mr. Herbert."

Nod.

"Cooling down some now, Mr. Herbert."

Another nod.

"Have a nice evening, Mr. Herbert."

Nod.

"You tell that wife of yours hello for me."

Nod.

Uncle Herbert was always anxious to get home at the end of the day to see Aunt Carrie and lay into a good meal. My Aunt Carrie, who was smarter than her husband, had already used her good sense to send a neighbor boy to the liquor store early in the day to get herself a fifth of whiskey. This daily lubricant fueled her housework, her many phone calls on behalf of her beloved Eastern Star fraternal organization, and her interesting dinner creations.

When we arrived, Aunt Carrie had bathed, perfumed, corseted, and coifed herself and had dinner ready for her two working people. After Uncle Herbert and I did a quick wash-up, we all sat down at a laden table. A lot of it was mystery dishes. I was a picky eater, but I usually couldn't resist trying the strange. (I was defeated once when Aunt Carrie served a baked animal of some sort, complete with head and feet and eyes. I think it might have been a muskrat. It looked rat-ish and big.) As we ate, Aunt Carrie and Uncle Herbert settled into their nightly rhythm, sharing news from their day and the latest gossip. I loved mealtimes. They were just the place for collecting material to think about and put in my journals.

After putting away the food, washing the dishes, and feeding Cousin Tommy, it was time for Aunt Carrie and Uncle Herbert to settle down to finish the last of their respective nips. They usually stayed in the kitchen to enjoy their after-dinner libations while I bathed and went to my room to read, eavesdrop, and daydream. Sometimes, though,

Uncle Herbert sat up late listening to the radio (with which he carried on animated conversations) and talking and cradling Cousin Tommy in a maudlin embrace. Those nights, I invented excuses to walk through the kitchen where I'd see him and the cat both progress from satisfaction to outright stupor.

On especially good nights, Aunt Carrie and Uncle Herbert would have themselves a set-to. This mostly occurred on weekends. It was loud, but it never got physical. Except one time when Aunt Carrie decided she'd had enough foolishness and pushed Uncle Herbert out of his chair, through the screen door, and down the back steps. What a sight! But, of course, I couldn't count on this good stuff happening with any regularity.

Most nights ended peaceably with their open-mouthed snores gentling me to sleep. I loved this protected cocoon, where I learned and grew and began to know myself and think the thoughts that are still mine today.

Aunt Carrie died when I was fifteen, and I lost touch with Uncle Herbert when I went to live with my mother and stepfather. But way before then, I had already practiced disappearing Aunt Carrie and Uncle Herbert from my mind and heart. Just in case.

# 3: A Child's Cold War

Each 9/11 anniversary propels me back in time to my own coming of age in a world suddenly declared unsafe. I grew up in an era in which the American psyche was subsumed by fear of an impending nuclear holocaust. Brinksmanship geopolitics between the United States and the then Soviet Union from 1946 to 1991—known as the Cold War—was one of the most determining factors in my young development.

I don't know whether it was better in the long run to experience, as I did, the drawn-out, drip-drip-drip anticipation of disaster or whether, like the children of 9/11, to be shocked by the unthinkable actually happening. I also don't know which is more impactful—visions of annihilation recurring in the imagination or being bombarded with an unending video loop of planes hitting the twin towers and close-ups of the zombie-shuffling survivors. For both generations, the result seems to have been the same—a clash of ideologies that leaped from ferocious rhetoric into scarifying reality. Everyone was affected. And we all began defining our lives in terms of before and after.

The geopolitics of the '50s and '60s prepared me to face uncertainty, to survive chaos, and to function in a world devoid of reassuring and familiar places, people, and things. In one way, the global threat armed me with tools that helped me survive a chaotic home life. On the one hand, I could be stoic and tamp down my feelings to the point where I had to work hard to find my true emotions. At the same time, I could be invested with an adventurous and sometimes-fearless spirit, since, after all, who knows if there'll be a tomorrow? It is almost second nature to put my feelings on a shelf to attend to the task at hand, a trait that stood me in good stead in my professional life. I am also one of the best people you could have around in an emergency. I still don't know when to ask for help when I need it. After all, being overly emotional and needy in the face of an impending World War III could mean the difference between survival and death. The Cold War officially ended in 1991, but by that time, I had been indelibly branded.

The Cold War harangue of annihilation that was on the lips of nearly all authority figures started my life-long habit of playing the "what-if" game, which required me to anticipate every possible negative thing that could happen in any given situation and to work out my response. "Preparedness" is still my mantra. For example, even though the closest I get to the wilderness is the suburban discount mall, my car is always packed with energy bars, a survival blanket, gloves, a signaling device, heavy shoes, and other emergency gear. Just in case. I have been in a state of emergency preparedness my whole life. Contrarily, I have conscientiously ignored all Homeland Security Department advisories to keep an emergency kit handy. Unlike "doomsday-preppers," I think I've decided that dying in the first strike is better than struggling to survive the unsurvivable.

I first became aware of the Cold War in second grade. It was a complete dash of cold water. I woke up to the realization that adults, of whom I had always been suspicious, were incapable of protecting me—or themselves—from harm. Some, like my husband, lived their entire childhoods blissfully unbothered by the nuclear threat and so maintained their confidence in the power and infallibility of adults. (I think this may be at the root of Bill's enviable optimistic outlook.) Perhaps my awareness of a less-secure world was more acute because my hometown abutted Fort Campbell, an Army base. The base was home to the renowned 101st Airborne Division (a.k.a. the "Screaming Eagles"), which was frequently deployed in response to some threat or international crisis. Only a few miles away was Fort Knox, where the nation's gold supply was stored. Local expectations were that both bases would be among the first targets of Soviet intercontinental ballistic missiles.

The year I was born, 1951, the Federal Civil Defense Administration produced the film "Duck and Cover," which was used right through the mid-1960s to terrify American school children about the threat of nuclear weapons. By the time I was in third grade, we had learned how, upon hearing the blast of the civil defense siren, to duck under our desks and cover our heads with a hankie(!) and retreat into a shell of protection—just like Bertie the Turtle did whenever he encountered danger. (Of course, no one told us that "duck and cover" hadn't worked for the Japanese when we bombed Hiroshima and Nagasaki in World War II.)

It seemed as though we saw the Bertie the Turtle film at least once a month. At other times, we had special classes in which we were taught about the different levels of radiation and their effects. Alpha radiation just tanned you and was mostly survivable. Gamma radiation meant you were burnt toast—literally. We also learned how to administer first aid and how to care for the few expected survivors who would be suffering from any number of fallout-related injuries. Citizens were advised to build bomb shelters and stock them with supplies to last through the first weeks of the disaster. Men were urged to arm themselves so they could fend off the hordes of the hungry, less-prepared citizenry. City leaders put signs on several buildings designating them as public shelters in case you were caught away from home.

 School children would be sheltered in the basements of their schools, or, if there were time, they would be sent home to die with their families.

You could be sitting at your third-grade desk concentrating on diagramming a sentence, writing

24

definitions to vocabulary words, taking a pop math quiz, or trying to surreptitiously pass a note.

The civil defense horn would jolt through the school. The whole class was startled. Some of the boys, as well as a few tough girls, would roll their eyes, faking bravado. Occasionally, a kid would wet himself. (It was always the same kid.) My insides would freeze up and start cracking like an ice cube thrown in boiling water. Mrs. Bacon, our teacher, would say calmly, "Children, you know what to do." At that, we'd fish out our hankies from our book satchels, kneel under our desks, and put the cloth over our heads. While crouching under our desks, some of us said our prayers, and the rest of us whispered to each other: "Do you think it's real this time?" The answer came only when we heard the all-clear signal, and our principal announced over the loudspeaker: "This has been a test." The only evidence of what we had endured was the dusty knees that we carried like Cold War medals throughout the rest of the day. Even though the drill was over, my mind still held images from those terrible movies of the time, which showed a future

Earth littered with uprooted, broken buildings and casually strewn, disfigured bodies. I never fully believed that it had all been a test until I returned home from school at the end of the day. Occasionally I wondered whether the enemy children also had knelt under their desks and were feeling the same as I.

For weeks after each drill, I expected to leave school and walk out into a world populated by destroyed buildings, no people, and no way to get back to those I loved. From the beginning, I decided that I would be one of the survivors. I was not going to die because I became too paralyzed or overwhelmed (like the women in those movies) to save myself. To make sure of this, I pre-grieved everyone and everything that I knew and loved. As a result, I wouldn't have to waste time on it when the "big one" dropped. I'd just switch smoothly into survival mode with all my wits about me. Movies such as "War of the Worlds" fed my young imagination with notions of mass destruction and a world turned upside down. I devoured any literature I could find that could tell me about the destruction the United States had visited upon Hiroshima and Nagasaki in World War II. By the time of the 13-day stand-off in 1962, known as the Cuban Missile Crisis, in which a Soviet-armed Cuba threatened retaliation against the U.S. for its role in the failed Bay of Pigs invasion, I was almost blasé. My peers, on the other hand, carried their worried faces into the classroom as homes emptied of fathers who were ordered back to Fort Campbell when the base went on high alert. The Cuban Missile Crisis has been widely acknowledged by historians as the closest we came in the Cold War to what was termed "Mutual Assured Destruction—MAD." By the time this happened, I was a veteran at how to cope with the unthinkable. The fact that the good sense of leaders on both sides prevailed was almost of no matter to me personally, though the children and adults around me let out their collectively held breaths. In 1968, when I was a jaded teenager, the movie "The Planet of the Apes" worked its way into popular culture, giving us a glimpse into one fanciful consequence of humankind's self-destructive urges. My duck-and-cover experience saw me through it all.

When the Berlin Wall came down on November 9, 1989, I felt that a big burden had been lifted. But now, 9/11, school shootings, increased Russian aggression, and the rise in domestic terrorism by radical whites has eroded that first aura of hope. I see loving, tolerant, and life-affirming people everywhere caught in the crosshairs. Some people of color would say that the target never moved away from us, just that more people have been added. One good thing is that the razor's-edge fear that we felt during the Cold War can't be sustained indefinitely. Another good thing has been the explosion of activism among young people around the world. That gives me hope. But I'm not forgetting my duck-and-cover lessons.

# 4: Integrating Hopkinsville

In 1954, the Supreme Court decided in the *Brown v. Board of Education* [of Topeka, Kansas] case that maintaining "separate but equal" schooling for blacks and whites was unconstitutional, and several high-profile desegregation cases ensued. In my hometown, Hopkinsville, desegregation—like everything else—took its own peculiar route. In our collective Kentuckian psyche, we tried to distinguish ourselves from "the South." This was the home of Abraham Lincoln, after all. Other favorite sons included Edgar Cayce, the famous psychic, and Ted Poston, the first black journalist to write for a major white U.S. newspaper. The city became well-known through Poston's many articles chronicling his youth. Hopkinsville is in Southwest Kentucky, near the Tennessee border, on the *nunna daul tsuny*, the "Trail Where They Cried," historically known as the Trail of Tears, the forced march of Cherokee Indians (and their black slaves) from northern Georgia to Oklahoma in 1838 and 1839. Several captives escaped, were hidden by blacks, and, like my great grandmother, married into the black community.

Like many small towns, Hopkinsville had its own power structure and social strata. The legacy of the Civil War was never far away. As a reward for siding with the Union, Kentucky was exempted from the Emancipation Proclamation, and only in 1976 did it formally ratify the

13th, 14th, and 15th amendments. (A friend told me there was actually debate on this!) Old-school Democrats, later known as "Dixiecrats," committed their energies to protecting the status quo (what I call "white over right"). A good many whites were secret (some not-so-secret) members of the Klan—"old Kluxers," as my grandfather called them. Instead of burning crosses, they wielded the whip of economic power to keep blacks in "their place." One major example was the City Council's ruling to keep Hopkinsville "safe" by discouraging soldiers stationed at the adjacent, racially-integrated Fort Campbell Army base from coming into town. I suspect at least a big part of the reason was the fear of unrest that would be caused as black soldiers demanded a level of respect and treatment that was not being accorded to black residents. The city succeeded and is still paying the economic costs. Republicans often referred to themselves as "the Party of Lincoln." The party gave blacks some of their first elective successes, including our deputy mayor and our first black school board member, my grandfather. Everything changed in 1960 when John F. Kennedy ran for president. Black Republicans became diehard Democrats, and "former" Klansmen became dedicated Republicans. Some, like my father's light-skinned, well-educated, wealthy family, remained loyal to the Republican Party, while others, like my mother's darkercomplected working-class family, rushed to join the Democrats, who promised a new social order.

In everyday life, most Hoptowners, as we were called, eschewed labels. We all knew each other, and we knew each other's secrets. We figured out our own way to co-exist. For example, the most racist among us also, at times, secretly supported liberal causes (as well as their half-black children). Also, select light-skinned blacks participated almost fully in white society, with everyone's knowledge and consent. Some, including members of my own family, gave up their dual existences and made a permanent move into the white world—in the north and west. They left their homes and families to disappear into the largely white worlds of Chicago, the District of Columbia, and California. We saw them on their yearly visits back to their black families.

The other power group was comprised of women, nearly all of them black, who were "in service" to powerful families, were accorded the highest levels of respect, and wielded great backdoor power. They could be counted on to counsel young women on which families were "nice" and which were to be avoided. Among the worst families were those in which the women, particularly young ones, would be risking abuse. My mother, who was college-educated, was in service for three years to the town's most powerful judge; this was a nice family. As a consequence, I spent many hours with his wife and children, taking advantage of the amenities at his restricted country club, and my family was exempted from Jim Crow. I guess that was a sort of "white by association" status. After three years, my mother was rewarded with an appointment to co-chair the local Democratic Party and, later, with a state civil service job.

In-service women were the main conduits for information and brokers of relations between the races. Whites conferred with their "girls" when blacks came to them to purchase property and businesses or to apply for loans. Likewise, blacks sought counsel from these "girls" about which whites would be most receptive to their proposals. These in-service women even weighed in on and helped mediate legal cases. They were among the first to realize that change was coming, and they took it upon themselves to make sure that black children were up to the challenge of competing in a white world.

My grandmother, Big Hattie (the best cook in town) teamed up with Mrs. W., our most sophisticated teacher, to start the "School of Comportment for Young Southern Ladies." Girls gathered in Mrs. W's large, formal dining room after school and on Saturdays to practice walking across the room balancing books on our heads; proper, ladylike, sitting with crossed ankles; how the well-bred young woman "addresses" a formal table-setting; how to choke down watercress sandwiches daintily; how to master proper elocution (in other words, talking "whiter than white"); and how to master other vital skills. Our teachers graduated us by hosting a dress-up dance (boys had to attend only one class in order to participate). Each graduate received a 20-volume set of miniature red leatherette books containing classics of American and English literature—which apparently was what they thought was exactly what we needed to hold our own in white society! Ironically, thus-equipped, we were better at being "white high society" than any of the white people in our town. It would take me nearly 20 years to actually use all these skills and to fully appreciate the gift given to me by these two women. (I still find it the rare person who knows how to properly use a fish knife.)

Attorney L.P. McHenry, the city's civil rights lawyer, channeled Thurgood Marshall, then a star attorney of the National Association for the Advancement of Colored People (NAACP). Town leaders respected and feared him. The in-service ladies adored him—"he looks so much like Reverend Martin Luther King," they said—so he always got information beforehand about his opponents' plans. Sometimes, just his threat of a lawsuit was enough to trigger changes. He did not make speeches or call for boycotts or marches, but the black community still looked to him to safeguard its interests. His fight for integration continued even after his death, when his family sued the city for the right to bury him in the white cemetery.

In 1958, he sent his six-year-old daughter, Linda, to become the first black child in our town to enroll in a white school. Indoctrinated by her father, Linda became a full-time emissary for her race. From the time she and I first met, we never talked about inconsequential things. It was always about the leading issues of the day, as though we knew we were to play a part. She was my first experience with a social-change warrior. We talked about her dream of becoming a lawyer like her father or a news commentator like Sander Vanocur. It was only when we were older and ushers at the Freeman Chapel A.M.E. Church that I learned of her struggles and triumphs—getting her turn at playground games; learning to never show fear or sadness; eating alone; finally having a teacher call on her and actually listen to her answer; scoring higher than everyone else on a quiz; ignoring whispered name-calling and other slights. The loneliness of being the first and only. We were close already, but these conversations cemented a lifelong friendship.

Attorney L.P. continuously lobbied black families, trying to convince them to send their children to white schools. Parents listened politely but were unswayed. Black people in Hopkinsville were rightly proud of their schools. White schools had more resources (we were recipients of the textbooks no longer used by white students), but few black parents were convinced they provided a superior education. Integration also meant separating children from teachers who knew them and their families intimately and who were vital members of the black community. Finally, parents were apprehensive about relinquishing their children to a harsh and potentially violent environment. Despite great effort, Attorney L.P. was able to convert only one family—mine.

In 1964, I left the all-black Booker T. Washington Elementary School and entered the newly-built Kaufmann Junior High School, where I was placed in the seventh grade "advanced" track. I had four things to protect me: my physician grandfather recently had been re-elected to the school board; my mother was politically active and "connected"; I was light-skinned and therefore was considered smart. Also, years of association with upper-class whites meant that most of the black culture and identity had been bleached away. In other words, I was whiter than most white people. Linda and I were the only black kids at our respective schools. Then, a year later, Linda joined me at Kaufmann. It was the just two of us—until Linda completed the eighth grade and I finished ninth.

While the integration fight was heating up in the South, it remained an angry undercurrent in our town. This was a time when Catholic priests and nuns were outspoken voices for social justice and were at the forefront of the civil rights movement. At one point, the Archbishop of Louisville issued a statement warning that any Catholics who opposed integration risked excommunication. On rare occasions, our local newspaper reported stories about sit-ins and school integration, and each time, they ran side-bar photos of Linda and me. I don't know if this was meant to offer hope or to remind folk that they should be scared. Midway through seventh grade, one of the teachers from my old school recruited me to act the part of Snow White in her class play. I still have the photo of my pale, long-haired self in costume surrounded by a group of darker-skinned fifth-graders. At the time, I was excited about being in a play. Now I wonder how those kids felt about their teacher thinking none of them was good enough (i.e., light-skinned) to be Snow White.

After a year of being the two "onlys" Linda and I were joined by four black kids who had come in from Saints Peter and Paul Catholic School. We all seemed to survive and thrive in our own way. Our lunch periods coincided, but we rarely sat together, as if "Negro" was a communicable disease. During my tenure in junior high, I learned to endure being pushed aside at the water fountain, play deaf to the few whispers of "nigger" as I passed in the hall, and control my kidneys until I got home. I was confused since, at that time, I was just as light as a lot of the white kids. Sometimes, kids and teachers assumed I was white. When this happened, I felt suddenly unburdened from my role as a symbol of integration. Relief was quickly replaced by fear of being "outed." I always was. I prayed for the gift of invisibility. I was *me*, not some "integration kid." Sometimes I wished I was light enough to live with my Chicago and D.C. cousins who "passed," but, as my family so often told me, I was "light and bright, but sadly, two drops from white."

One day, in study hall, where we were supposed to keep quiet, Jenny, the golden daughter of a well-known town doctor, came up to me, acting as though she had nothing to fear from the study hall monitor.

"Hi," she said.

I whispered hello. "I'm Vikki."

She was blonde and tan and everything that everyone else wanted to be, and she knew that she was the best and brightest of us. Her parents had taken her to Europe and spent lavishly on tennis and riding lessons and had laid out nearly a thousand dollars for her braces (as she kept telling us). We all wanted to be her—or at least imitate her confidence—so once she acknowledged me, it was imperative that everyone else do the same. Jenny and I ate together, traded answers in study hall, and teamed up for French class. For the first time, white kids envied me, though they struggled visibly with how to be "in" with Jenny while holding on to the prejudices of their parents. Some simply created the fictional belief that, despite well-known fact, I couldn't possibly be black since I talked, looked, and acted like them.

In ninth grade, a close friend, Karen, came to my house after school. (I was living with my great aunt and uncle.) We did our homework together on the dining room table, had a snack, and talked about which boys were cutest until it was time for my aunt and me to walk her back to school, where she was to meet her mom for the ride home. I never dreamed it would be the last time I'd see her. She wasn't in school the next day or the ones that followed. I later learned that her mom had been so upset at seeing us together that her parents had pulled her out of school and sent her to live with relatives in Ohio. We never got to say goodbye. I couldn't cry about it. It was just the way things were. Sometime later, I visited a schoolmate's home. His mother welcomed me and chatted with us as we ate our snacks. When we finished eating, she continued smiling and talking amiably as she put her son's dishes in the sink and mine in a brown paper bag, which she folded neatly at the top. Soon, it was time for me to leave, and she walked me to my aunt's car, where she praised my manners and announced she was so happy her son and I were friends. As we began to drive off, I chattered on about my great afternoon but stopped when I saw my friend's mother gently deposit the brown bag in the garbage can on her way back to the house. That was when I understood the power and danger I posed. School was school, and home was home, two countries at stalemate like the USSR and the United States. Although I had met Jenny's mother and father several times, I made sure that I never visited her home. These incidents played over and over as I watched my white friends actually believe and act on church platitudes, only to be blindsided by their parents' hypocrisy and racism.

In 1966, the city closed the all-black Crispus Attucks High School, which taught seventh- through twelfth-graders, and forced its students to attend Kaufmann Junior High and Hopkinsville High School. Hopkinsville High School, or HHS, as it was called, operated like an elite private school. Classes were more likely segregated by income than academic ability. The mighty PTA members offered their wealthy children access to riding lessons and golfing at the country club and even went so far as to pay for an Olympic-sized pool for the swim team. Everybody who was anybody went to HHS. My classmates buzzed with rumors about what integration would mean. They were fearful, and so was I. When Jenny casually announced, "My parents are going to send me to private school as soon as the Attucks kids come," it was like being hit with a bucket of very cold spit. I struggled to remain expressionless and willed myself not to hear any more. It stunned me that my friends had also absorbed the racism of their parents.

As news of the impending integration of HHS spread, the uproar in the city grew. Meanwhile, I had my own doubts. What if the niche that I had carved for myself was disturbed? In my three years at Kaufmann, I had lost the connection and ability to deal comfortably with black kids, and I wasn't far along in figuring out white ones.

As I began tenth grade at HHS, only six black students were added to my college-track classes. They were nice, but I no longer was skilled or confident enough to make friends. I was used to sitting with my white friends. These were the so-called "radicals," in '60s parlance, but it soon became clear that I was expected to declare my allegiance and sit with black students whom I did not know. It was a caste system worse than the ones in India and South Africa, and I was in the middle. The college-track black kids mingled easily with kids from their old school. White kids also clamored for their attention. They moved between groups with an ease that I did not understand. Years of learning and being nurtured in an all-black environment had given them a level of confidence and self-perception that I lacked. They became "stars" and were loved by teachers and students alike for their talents. I was as smart as they were, but I just couldn't crack the code. I envied them. Suddenly, I, who had spent three years in this life, no longer had any standing or credibility. Black students laughed at how I talked ("white"), my ignorance of black slang, dancing, and other aspects of black culture. There were few opportunities to learn. My mother disdained casual contact with people whom she considered "common." "Common" usually included poor, working-class people of any race or dark-skinned blacks— all attributes that described her.

I wish I could say I was politically aware, but I wasn't. Oh, I knew what was happening, but I just exiled it to some dark corner of my brain. I spent a lot of time in the city library, where I struggled to comprehend the writings of Anais Nin, Henry Miller, Collette, and the newly discovered Richard Wright. I daydreamed about fitting in and promised myself that my day would come.

# 5: The Little Red Books

When I was in the ninth grade, talk swirled about the closing of the black high school. Crispus Attucks. Attucks had been a fixture in Hopkinsville for nearly a century. There were strong emotions on both sides. Blacks feared for their children going to the then-all-white Hopkinsville High School (HHS). Black parents were reluctant to hand their children over to noncaring white teachers since only a few of the black educators would make the transition to HHS.

I never went to Attucks, yet I couldn't escape the talk. I was in my third year at the formerly white junior high school. My so-called friends, all white, talked hysterically about the coming change. My closest friend declared her parents were sending her to private school rather than exposing her to an integrated high school. I remember her words and inflection to this day.

The summer before I was to enter high school, I got a present of 50 small (3"x4") red leatherette books. The Baptist preacher, Reverend Louis, got these books from some unknown source and disseminated them to lots of us in his zeal to ensure black kids would be able to compete in the hostile white environment. The attitude that white kids were better (at almost everything, with the exception of music) permeated the black community. Despite having white friends, my mother never lost her conviction that white people were somehow superior. The women who were in

42

service already knew that wealthy white families had more but were not necessarily smarter. Their efforts with us centered on making sure we were exposed to different foods, manners, and ease at being in new social situations. (It took being in college before many of us were actually invited to integrated social events.) Reverend Louis' concern was more substantive. In his view, black children had been disadvantaged from years of poor schooling and having access only to schoolbooks already used and marked up by whites. Kentucky never gave black children new or updated texts. When I entered junior high school, I was shocked and delighted to be given a brand new textbook.

The red books were one way to make black kids even when they went to HHS. The titles included all the classics in poetry and literature, such as:

- Essays of Emerson
- The Gold Bug by Poe
- Fifty Best Poems of America
- Courtship of Miles Standish by Longfellow
- Lots of Shakespeare

Although I was already an integration pioneer, I got a set of books as well. I cherished them and read them all during summer break. I still have 30 of these gems and often put one in my purse when I know I will have to wait, such as at the doctor's office. You can still find them on eBay or other sites.

There have been several versions of these little books, beginning with the genuine leather ones published by the Little Leather Library Corporation in 1915. The little books were used as bonuses for marketing products, including cigarettes, among other things. Ownership changed hands in 1924. The next new edition bore the name "Little Luxart Library" and was published by Robert K. Haas, Inc. until 1925. By then, they were no longer in use, so, typically, they were available to be owned by black people, i.e., Reverend Louis. They were a decent, thoughtful link to the past and to the efforts of people like Reverend Louis (and those women in service) to ensure that black kids could succeed.

As usual, we overdid it. We over-estimated the smarts of white kids. When we finally got to HHS, we knew so much more than they. Still, few black kids made it into the college track, though some were so smart that their brilliance could not be suppressed. It was still a fight to get them recognized. Even when two black boys at my high school won prestigious Rhodes scholarships, they were still treated as second-class students. In contrast, much was made of a white boy in my class who was deemed a genius and granted early admission to Vanderbilt University. Go figure.

# 6: The Fighting Tigers Band

The main racial-mixing pot at Hopkinsville High School besides the football and basketball teams, was the Fighting Tigers Band. With a year of clarinet lessons under my belt, I was ready. I arrived at HHS at the same time as our band leader, Mr. MacCauley. His reputation had preceded him. He was known for his punishing practice sessions and intolerance of racial bias that he applied equally to kids and adults. No apologies. A few white parents withdrew their children from the band. Too bad for them. Under Mac's leadership, we became a family. We were his, we loved him, and we were *fierce*!

We drilled and practiced in rain, cold, heat, and late after-school. Parents complained, but we were the first ones to defend this grueling schedule, even though we were exhausted. Mac taught us that we could go beyond ourselves. We became the best. (In truth, we were pretty mediocre, but you couldn't tell us that.) When we took the field at half-time, we owned it! When we donned our orange-and-black letter sweaters, we received instant respect at school. Band members walked with a special swagger—not as hip as the in-the-know black kids, but still, it was our own. We wore our sweaters with special pride. (I still have mine.) *Make way when we come through! We're Fighting Tigers!* To us, the band was more than an extra-curricular activity; it was who you were. This unity enabled us to make history.

In 1967, Mac got us a gig marching in a special parade in Pensacola, Florida. The invitation came at a time when the South was "ground zero" for the modern civil rights movement, which began in 1955 when Rosa Parks became the second black woman to refuse to give up her bus seat to a white passenger. The Freedom Riders of the 1960s were in full swing, and three civil rights workers were lynched in Mississippi in 1964 during Freedom Summer. In 1965 America was treated to "Bloody Sunday," the brutal televised images of police attacking peaceful marchers who were bringing their civil rights message from Selma, Alabama, to Montgomery. These all presaged the very real potential for violence, especially in the South, at even the appearance of an integrated group like our band.

All this swirled in the back of our minds but did nothing to dampen our excitement at the honor of the invitation and the prospect of a trip to Florida. We didn't think beyond that. Others did, and they were worried. In the band room, our main concern was that adults would intervene to cheat the Fighting Tigers out of the reward we had earned. They warned us that "this type of thing"—that is, taking a mixed-race band through the South—had not been done before. Parents talked about the dangers and the "what-ifs" over the dinner table, at church, at PTA meetings, and with us. Mac began his rounds, bringing us together in groups—full band, black band members (all 12 of us), parents, even city officials. Each step of the way, we won them over. The Fighting Tigers would march in Pensacola!

To most of us, Florida was just the finger-shaped state at the end of the U.S. We didn't know much about geography, but we knew we had to travel through Southern states to get there. All the black kids had heard their parents' voices fill with awe and fear when they said the word "Mississippi." "Mississippi" was the evil monster that could drag us from our beds and devour us. "Alabama" was another monster. There were no defenses. Our parents, relatives, and neighbors offered up stories of their battles. We were smug in the knowledge that we were living in a different time. We were the Fighting, Fierce Tigers, and Mac was our leader. We weren't afraid. What happened to one happened to all. We would be safe as long as we were together.

Each day at school and at band practice, we talked about the impending trip and the wonderful things we would see. Our enthusiasm stayed at a level of frenzy that can be sustained only by teenagers. Gladys, a flutist, shared copies of *Jet* magazine featuring beautiful, black, swimsuit-clad Florida co-eds. James, a percussionist, brought in his father's AAA map so we could trace our route. White girls engaged in earnest discussions about sun-tanning. Each day someone tossed a new "fact" in the rumor mill. Mac passed out a brochure from our hotel featuring photos of exotic food platters (with lobster!) and of people laughing as they tossed beach balls and frolicked in the surf. It was hard to comprehend a place where it was always sunny and warm and where the beach was an everyday part of life.

A few parents wanted to pay for their kids' expenses, but Mac vetoed the idea, saying it would cause a rift between wealthy and poor kids in the band. We would raise all our funds as a group from bake sales, car washes, special collections, gifts from civic groups, and other enterprises. We kept a running total, which we announced each week until the money was finally raised. After constantly checking with each other about the appropriate thing to take, we packed them, re-packed them, and packed them again. Black kids were embarrassed about carrying additional packages containing food, but our folks were adamant, saying they knew things about traveling in the South that we didn't. We hid these packages away and hoped that we would prove their experiences a lie.

Our route would take us 450 miles from Hopkinsville through Tennessee, Mississippi, and Alabama, before ending in Florida. Instead of school buses, we would ride the twelve hours in style on buses with plush seats and toilets, and we'd have plenty of time to test being a family. I was both eager and scared. Besides traveling in a large group, I would be sharing a hotel room in a strange city with three of my bandmates, all black. My interpersonal skills were few, and I worried that my roommates would discover my differentness.

The day of departure came, and we straggled into the early morning parking lot, hunching down into our coats against the wind. Only a few people came to see us off. The principal was there. We quickly stored our instruments and luggage and boarded our assigned buses. The engines started, and we were off.

An hour out, we sailed through Nashville, then turned south. Conversation tapered off, and we settled into the monotony of the road. By the time the buses pulled into Bob's Big Boy in Decatur, Mississippi, we were ready to get out, walk on solid ground, and eat. Mac led us into the restaurant, where we sat at tables, segregating ourselves like always by the instruments we played rather than race. We sat talking and making jokes, not noticing that the restaurant had grown quiet. New diners—all white—came in, got their food, ate, and left. The black kids stared at each other until Darryl finally stood up. "No sense making everybody starve." With that, he walked out the door, followed quickly by the rest of us. Back on the bus, we avoided looking at each other as we opened our food packs and ate, for once thankful for our parents' paranoia. Reggie muttered between bites, "who wants to eat with peckerwoods anyway?" We nodded, but I know that each of us longed to be in the restaurant with our friends. Some kids kept vigil at the windows, hoping to see Mac and the rest of the band members coming to join us. They arrived about an hour later, and we separated onto our assigned buses. The atmosphere on my bus was tense and silent until Braxton, one of the regular cut-ups, started describing the "hillbillies" in the restaurant. The rest of the white band members joined in, speaking all over themselves about the people and how awful the food was. I couldn't say anything. It felt like I was hearing it all from underwater. The black kids turned accusatory eyes on Mac. He said nothing, but for the first time ever, he refused to make eye contact. It was the only time I ever saw him look hound-dog and defeated. "This won't happen again," he said quietly. Our eyes said, "we'll see," as we stoically settled in for the rest of the trip.

The buses rolled through Birmingham, Mississippi, and in a few hours, we reached the Alabama border. At Montgomery, Mac had the buses pull over in front of a church. He got off and went inside, then came back and talked to the bus drivers. When he re-boarded, we set off on a circuitous trip through narrow residential streets, ending in the parking lot of a large church. We got out, were greeted by a minister, and led through a side door decorated with the sign, "Free Meals—Everyone Welcome." Mac was feeding us at a soup kitchen for vagrants and drunks! Our group was subdued as we trouped in and sat down. We went through the food line, trying not to stare at the disreputable-looking folk who were busy wolfing down enormous trays of food. Soon, we relaxed and began eating the delicious array. The food was satisfying, but more importantly, the staff and other customers came by to ask who we were, where we were going, and to bless us. Mac had done his magic again. The more we relaxed, the more I tried to make myself forget Decatur. I didn't completely succeed, but I tried.

As I returned my tray and got ready to leave, a mound of rags with feet approached and touched my arm lightly. "It's a good thing you kids are doing. Good luck in Florida." I didn't know whether to feel blessed or offended at the nearness of this kind bum, but years of training in politeness took over, and I mumbled some kind of reply. Back on board the buses, it was a clear shot from Montgomery to Mobile and then just a jump to Pensacola.

Our arrival in Pensacola was anti-climactic. The weather was nice, but all we felt was cramped and tired. The beach was nowhere to be seen, and the hotel was just a large, square building with a cavernous lobby. We half-listened to the instructions about our schedule. All we knew was that we had actually done what we set out to do—we had traveled from Hopkinsville, Kentucky, to Pensacola, Florida. That was as much as we could absorb at this point. Even our adolescent energy failed us.

Linda, Gladys, Phyllis, and I gathered our stuff and went to our assigned room. We opened the door and looked in on an over-furnished room in which everything was some variation of beige. "You can't tell the furniture from the walls from the carpet," said Phyllis.

I tried to sound reassuring. "It's only for tonight."

With a collective sigh, we nudged each other into the room and began claiming our space, two to a bed. Silently, we unpacked and took turns washing up. It felt like church. We hurried back to the lobby to meet up with the rest of the band.

The hotel had been prepared for us—had they been warned? Dinner was uneventful—not as welcoming as our lunch in Montgomery, but definitely a step up from Decatur. A taciturn and disinterested staff served us all in turn, and after we ate, we gathered in the lobby to hear rallying speeches from Mac and from Bobby, our drum major. They went on and on about how proud we should be, how historic this trip was, and how we were going to show everybody up the next day. It was time to retire and prepare for the big day.

While we took turns bathing and completing bedtime rituals, I kept waiting for someone to bring up Decatur and Montgomery, but no one did. The intimate smells of Ivory soap, Nivea skin oil, Noxzema face cream, and hair pomade mingled comfortingly as we prepared for bed. Soon we had climbed into our private worlds and sleep.

In the morning, we repeated our nighttime preparations, only in reverse. "I hope nobody acts ugly," Gladys said. No one answered, but we all knew what "acting ugly" meant—white folks throwing things or yelling "nigger" as we marched by. It was the word we had been hiding from since the beginning of the trip. It was the word we were holding our breath and straining to hear but hoping not to.

"We'll all be together." I tried to encourage us, though Decatur kept nagging at my mind.

The other girls smiled at each other as if to say I didn't have a clue. We all knew that the presence of Mac or our other band mates could not un-speak or undo "ugly" acts and words. We had to rely on our uniforms and ourselves to make us invulnerable. Sitting on the bus in our uniforms, we told ourselves we were the smartest, toughest, and best there was. I just hoped it would be enough.

At the parade grounds, we gave the once-over to other bands and pitied them for not being us. Minor catastrophes, a broken strap, and a lost cymbal—along with ample fidgeting—took up our time. We also noticed that other bands wore uniforms appropriate to the Florida heat while we stewed in our heavy wool. Soon we were off, marching behind a float. There were no friendly faces in the crowd, but we didn't see any outright hostile ones either. Mac strode beside us in his usual rumpled way, concentrating on something unseen. Finally, we got the cue! Horns up. Eyes ahead. Step big. Step proud. How we played, our polished instruments reflecting the sun and swaying in rhythm. The drum major stepped high and reared back nearly double. The crowd seemed to be with us, but we were caught up in our own glory and didn't need them. When we finished our number, we stole smug looks at one another. Our pride was so thick you couldn't wade through it. Mac was smiling and nodding his head. Despite the sweltering heat, we were marching on air!

Returning to the parade grounds, we were sweaty, tired, and grinning. After breaking down our equipment and storing our instruments on the buses, we went back to the hotel to collect our luggage. We stored our bags, ate, boarded our buses, and headed toward home.

# 7: Fast Girls

Fast girls were my high school *sheroes*. They stood out, didn't care, and smirked knowingly at the rest of us. They broke the rules and made new ones of their own. Offering no blind obedience to adults, they voiced questions that the rest of us had been too well-trained to ask. Teachers gave them passing respect. When fast girls asked questions, teachers struggled to provide real answers beyond those printed in the textbooks. Hecklers and taunters relished being put in their places by sharp tongues and saucy smiles. Just by their being, they gave the rest of us permission to discover a bit more about ourselves. I studied and admired fast girls. I started each school day with two who were in my homeroom.

\*\*\*

I like homeroom. Whoever invented it really understood the need for time to collect yourself before plunging into the school day, with all its changing teachers and classes and subjects and lock-step obedience to the bell. It was also the first time I got to see Lucie and Marsha, our so-called "fast girls."

Everybody in my homeroom was smart and college-bound. (We'd been tracked this way since junior high.) We were ambitious, eager to please, and imagined futures for ourselves beyond Hopkinsville. We were also mostly "good" kids, or what passed for such in Hopkinsville. (All of us girls wanted to be known as "good," which meant no all-the-way sex, no running around—in other words, not "fast.") We were the class officers, debate club members, editors, and yearbook staffers, and the ones who often were allowed to leave class to participate in outside activities. Despite our sameness, there still were cliques—athletes, who were the heroes of the school; popular girls, who were mostly girlfriends of the athletes; super-smart kids, who enjoyed notoriety as well as membership in the popular group; quiet, studious kids like me, who participated but weren't really part of the "in" crowd; and, finally, there were the "fast girls," who just charted their own course.

This Monday morning, I am sitting in my seat, pretending to review homework but really listening to everything. Newt, our star quarterback, is huddled at the back of the rooms with his teammates. They are laughing, kidding each other, and making crude jokes about something that happened at the weekend party at Linda's parents' lake house. The popular girls are all standing near the window, telling their own versions of stories from the party. This is the first I even heard there was a party. The popular kids are my sometimes friends because I am with them in the band and in the student newspaper. I never get a party invitation. Everyone knows my mother is so strict that "no" is the only answer I can give to any invitation.

The bell rings, and everyone moves, still talking, to their assigned seats, which are arranged alphabetically. I've spent the last four years looking at the back of Mary Ellen's head. The sameness is comforting. This year she went with a shortcut, and I discovered the mole on the right side of her neck. Each time I see it, it's like I've just discovered it for the first time.

Lucie and Marsha stroll in a couple of minutes after the bell. Their entrance punches a hole of silence in the general buzz of voices as the rest of the class marks their arrival and slowly digests their outfits. The girls in my class have more or less the same look: Pringle sweaters, cashmere sets, demure just-above-the-knee skirts, flats, hair that's on the restrained side of big, tasteful make-up, and a dainty piece of jewelry. Lucie and Marsha shake up the look with their own style, which seems to announce that they either are on the way to or just coming from a party. The rest of us live in the teenage illusion that we are grown, but they are the ones who look and act like real women.

Lucie is deep chocolate-colored and slender but with the beginnings of woman curves. Her clothes come mostly from the thrift store. We know this because a few of the girls have loudly recognized their once-owneds. Somehow, though, Lucie puts them together in a way never imagined by their previous owners. Today, she is wearing a very short red plaid pleated skirt that flares as she moves, topped with a bright yellow blouse (too bright for school), unbuttoned just enough to make the boys strain to look. She's a walking fiesta, with long, sparkling necklaces and multiple bracelets running up each arm. Crowning it all is the trademark blond streak that parts her processed hair from top to bottom on the right side. Lucie doesn't just walk—she struts to some inner music, her coltish legs leading just like those models on the runway.

Just a few paces behind is Marsha, coffee au lait and fleshier than Lucie. She strolls lightly on her feet, which are always encased in black fishnet stockings and two-inch heels—shoes that the rest of us girls are just being permitted to wear on Sundays. These are dead giveaways to her fast-girl status. Marsha shops at Cayce's, the best women's clothing store in town. She buys the basics like the rest of us but dares convention by adding lots of bracelets, scarves, and big earrings. On the surface, Marsha appears quieter than Lucie, but she often is the instigator of their adventures. She is smug and confident in the way well-off girls can be.

I think it's attitude more than the clothes that makes these two stand out. Their walks and looks throw out unspoken taunts: "We know something you don't know" and "you're all just too young to be let in on the secret." Or worse: "You're all sheep." Even the teachers feel it. Instead of the unquestioning obedience they are used to getting, our teachers have learned to be challenged by Lucie or Marsha, who demand that they justify their statements and commands. More than anything else, this confident questioning is what really puts Lucie and Marsha on near-equal footing with adults and inspires awe (and not a little bit of envy) in the rest of us.

***

Fourth period. American History. It's right after lunch, and the air is heavy with the efforts of all but a few of us to stay awake. Mr. Burrus is droning on, tossing in a few slangs trying to show he's hip, but it does just the opposite. My eyes settle to half-mast, and my body is playing hide-and-seek with sleep. In regular succession, my head bows slowly toward my chest until I'm almost gone, then jerks up suddenly awake. My pencil drags itself across the page automatically. When I go back to these class notes later, I'll laugh at the hieroglyphs.

All of a sudden, I notice the air sparkling with energy.

"Mr. Burrus, if the United States is all-powerful, why are we always so scared of everybody?"

Huh? What's going on? I missed what brought this on, but I'm at full attention now. So is the rest of the class.

"Lucie, I don't know what you mean. With the exception of the Indians, our early settlers weren't afraid of anything. Now, I really want to hear questions and comments about the early settlers."

"I don't mean just those pioneers, Mr. Burrus," Lucie continues with polite conviction. "I mean, all along, even now, we always have to have something to be afraid of. I can understand being afraid of the Indians—I mean, they're right there, and you've already seen them kill people, and you already know they want to kill you for stealing their land. But then later, men got afraid of women voting, President Roosevelt said we should be afraid of Japanese-Americans, everybody said the world should be afraid of Castro and the Soviets, and now whites got afraid of blacks. "

"We don't have time in this period to really talk about all those things," Mr. Burrus responds tiredly. "In the next chapters, some of this will come up, and we'll be exploring all the factors that result in—we don't call it fear—we say conflict. But for right now, we need to move on with the rest of today's lesson."

"Mr. Burrus?"

"Yes, Marsha?" Mr. Burrus sighs resignedly.

"It seems to me, there's just no point in being the biggest and baddest country in the world if all you're going to do is be afraid," Marsha says, refusing to relinquish this new area of questioning.

"Well, yes . . . I know. These are complex concepts that are a bit difficult for you to understand at your level, but now—"

Charles interrupts with bravado. "Seems to me, you being our teacher means you should be able to explain it so we can understand. Isn't that what education is about?"

"Class, that's enough!" Mr. Burrus says forcefully. "Let me give you your next assignment. We've run out of time. The bell's about to ring."

Lucie and Marsha cut eyes at each other, having accomplished their mission. The rest of us look down and smile as we write down our assignments. When the bell rings, we gather our things and leave, thankful that we were present when something interesting happened in class.

Lucie and Marsha have been each other's best friend since grade school. I don't know what brought them together, but what happens to one happens to the other. They don't need anybody else, and each looks only to the other for approval. They're smart and get good grades like the rest of us, but they act like they suspect our teachers of trying to hide the truth about things. They talk like they're following a curriculum that can't be found in our textbooks. They tell the stories passed down by the old folks in the black community. The rest of us believe what we're told—or, if we don't, we're too polite to say so.

We repeat rumors we've heard from our parents: "They go out to nightclubs." "Lucie has a boyfriend who is old enough to work at the Phelps-Dodge plant." "Somebody said Marsha's sister is really her daughter." "They play cards and gamble with those old boys who ride the loud motorcycles." Boys try to get a rise out of them, already anticipating the put-down, accompanied by the woman-laugh. Guys swell their chests at the sass from these two that would mean break-up if it came from the mouths of their girlfriends.

Lucie and Marsha act like they are just tolerating school, doing well, but with the understanding that real life resides somewhere else. They don't mind being seen at lunch or after school with lighted cigarettes. (Kentucky is a tobacco-producing state, and smoking is almost a civic duty.) I know other girls smoke, but they are careful to hide it. Most won't admit to it and certainly never carry cigarettes or matches in their purses. (If they do, they are quick to say they are carrying them for their boyfriends.)

Even when the hallway is crowded between classes, it's easy to pick out Lucie and Marsha. Besides the way they look, they are nearly always together, carrying their books loosely to the side, their hips rhythmic as they move unhurriedly to the next class. They share all but one class. When I'm real lucky, I catch them in the girls' restroom. Then I try to linger as long as I can, watch them tease their hair, re-apply make-up, and share a cigarette. They talk real fast in their own particular short-hand:

"You know, Mrs. Broadbent had the nerve to ask me if my momma saw how I dress coming to school," said Lucie, intent on adding a new layer of mascara.

"That old biddy looks like one of those schoolmarms you see on *Bonanza*."

"Ain't *that* the truth." Lucie turns to give Marsha some skin.

"I bet she's never had any," Marsha laughs wickedly.

"That's killing, girl," Lucie says, giggling.

Marsha changes the subject. "I can't wait to get to Mr. Redwine's class today. We start in cutting on our frogs."

"I bet it'll be the boys who turn out to be squeamish."

"Yeah."

Lucie, excitedly: "Ronald says he knows how to get us into the Ibex Club this Friday night."

"Well, I'll be cocked and ready." Marsha takes her turn at the mirror. With an appraising look and quick pat of her hair, she continues: "Let's get going. You know we have to make our entrance."

Since today there are a bunch of us girls in the restroom, I think some of this exchange is for our sakes. We pretend not to notice. If there are only a few girls around, Lucie and Marsha might give a little nod to let us know that they understand our longing and that offering up their conversation is just their way of taking pity on us. When it's just me in there with them, I hide and eavesdrop from the far stall. Lucie and Marsha, believing they are alone, then usually talk about how they are going to be roommates in college and live far away from our hometown.

And so, throughout the school day, I keep myself attuned to them.

***

Our parents warn us to stay away from them: "Those girls are just too fast. You'll get a reputation if you hang around them." Just the thing to make me want to be granted entry into their world.

After a whole day of fast-girl-watching, I walk out of the school building, clutching my books tightly to my chest, startled to feel a little sway in the movement of my hips. My insides would smile all over—until I came to my senses and realized I wasn't doing at all what a good girl should.

At home, in my bedroom, I test out being a fast girl. Hair piled up, skirt hitched, a straw "cigarette" dangling from my lips, I strike provocative poses and test out sharp comebacks. My mother too soon arrives home from work, and I am instantly transformed into the good girl who is tongue-tied around boys and unable to dish with the girls.

***

It's been nearly half a century since I last saw Lucie and Marsha, but I still am indebted to them. Thanks to them, this fast-girl wannabe had the courage to leave Hopkinsville and leap right into the biggest fast-girl club of the 1970s—the women's movement. I have channeled my inner fast-girl at so many important points in my life: my first civil rights demonstration; my first moot court and oral argument; lobbying congressmen; exhorting groups to take up an issue; then, deciding to leave it all for a more soul-nourishing lifestyle. So, to the fast girls of my youth, a belated thank-you. I owe you.

# 8: A Very Margaret Christmas[1]

It is Christmas Eve. The day has been a tumult of activity. I am in 11th grade, and it is the second year I have lived with my mother, Margaret, and stepfather, AB. (I have called her Margaret instead of Mother since I could talk, and she has never objected.) I see, early on, that this Christmas will be the same tragic comedy as the last. Margaret and I spent the morning going from store to store, trying on and buying clothes and shoes. Back home, the man (from Margaret's vast network) brought a large tree which Margaret decorates while also cooking an enormous feast of ham and greens and yeast rolls and yams and who knows what else. It is my job to work with her to wrap all we have bought into "presents" that will be arranged under the tree, photo-shoot style. I am drafted to make a caramel cake—my one domestic specialty. Every time Margaret goes to the kitchen or gets on the phone, I duck away from the frenzy for a brief serving of quiet. It's never long enough.

I am girding myself for how I know all this will end. AB has not come home for tonight's dinner and house trimming as he promised. He is off somewhere engaged in his chosen profession—gambling. He will be locked in until the game is over. If he's losing, he has to stay to win back his stake. If he's winning . . . well, why quit? I am required to bear

---

[1] First published as "Christmas" under the name Carter in <u>Christmas in My Mind,</u> by The Walsh Street Writers, 2012.

witness to this holiday ritual that has played out many times before, where my mother's desire for the perfect event crashes against disappointing reality.

By nine o'clock, the worm of reality has begun eating its way into Margaret's fantasy. I know this because her decorating-wrapping-cooking takes on an increasingly manic edge. She traverses the small house in angry, heavy pacing, and she begins to mutter louder and louder—to herself, to me, to the invisibilities.

"Nobody cares anything about family or being together on a holiday—and this is Jesus' birthday."

"I'm the only one who cares and who is willing to work."

"They'd better be happy and surprised with their presents—or else!"

I watch mutely as the play unfolds, hoping she doesn't turn on me. Foolish hope.

She finally notices me. "Why can't you be happy? You have everybody doing everything for, and you can't be anything but an ungrateful little brat." If I had the nerve, I'd say the same to her, but I remain silent. "You're just like your father! I don't see him here trying to make Christmas for you."

This last is her ultimate insult. She has conveniently forgotten the shopping trips with my father for school clothes and that he is buying nearly all my presents. She doesn't mention her rebuff of his invitation for me to come to the celebration at his parents' home. I have enough survival skills not to point this out.

As it nears midnight, Margaret steps up her agitated pacing, now adding a prop—a tightly clenched kitchen knife. Her rants are interspersed with brief crying jags. I am useless and make myself scarce. AB finally arrives. It was a good night, and he has won big, and he enters the living room easy-gaited and dapper. He greets Margaret in his soft, lazy-tongued way, smiling like a kid as he presents her with a diamond necklace. She pauses and delights over the offering before quickly ratcheting up her anger—this time directed at him. A quiet-spoken man, AB mostly listens, offering explanations that would be reasonable to anyone else. He reminds her she knew what she was getting into by marrying a gambler. Something is obviously wrong with the man thinking he can counter craziness with sanity. At least I am not off duty and can check out for the night.

Margaret wakes the household right after sunrise on Christmas morning. AB and I would rather sleep in. Why isn't she tired? She floats around, all engulfed in fluffy petals of rose-colored chiffon. By the time AB and I present ourselves, the dining room table is set with Christmas-themed china, crystal glasses, and laden platters. The powerful smell of food does its trick, and we are now fully awake. AB and I heap fervent praise on Margaret as we load up our plates. More, more, more, she urges us to eat. Having just one serving must mean something is wrong with the food, or you don't like it. When it becomes physically impossible to ingest another morsel, AB and I are herded into the living room to stare in awe at the exquisitely decorated Christmas tree and lights. Margaret and AB settle together on the sofa. It is the one moment of peaceful goodness that most resembles television families in an otherwise scary kaleidoscope.

It is my turn to be center stage, but I am still moving a bit slowly. Showing a flash of last night's anger, Margaret orders me to open my presents. I am supposed to play the guessing game, holding the package and remarking, "I wonder what this could be!" Margaret is irritated I am not showing the appropriate level of surprise and enthusiasm. I try, but I am not a very good actress. When I fall short, Margaret demands I re-wrap the present and do it all over again. I learn to be enthusiastic on cue. I want only to get my part over with, so I can return to my books and bed. The only present that is actually new is a shirt, necktie, and tie clip that she had wrapped at the store. She presents that as a gift to AB from both of us. He doesn't have a present for Margaret under the tree—assuming, silly man, that the diamond necklace he gave her last night sufficed. He quickly sees his mistake. As amends, he offers up plans for them to go out that evening for a night of music and dancing and show her off to all their friends—who have been trained over the years to act like they are eaten up with envy over her beauty, her outfit, her everything. By the end of the day, the tree is dismantled, the "presents" stowed away, and all traces of this Christmas are gone. Whew! Got through another one.

# 9: Whitehood

*White, you're alright*

*Yellow, you're mellow*

*Brown, stick around*

*Black, get back*

I was around five or six years old when I first heard this ditty. It was about the same time I learned the macabre child's singsong, "Ring Around the Rosies." Unfortunately, that first one was the hierarchical anthem that defined my environment—my family as well as the larger black community in Hopkinsville.

Though often laced with put-downs, my family took a not-so-secret delight in my light skin. My mother would idly gaze at me and express mock concern. "Ooh, that girl is so white it looks like she doesn't have any blood. Wonder if we should take her to the doctor?" My grandmother, upon her return from a trip downtown with me and my cousin, grumbled as she sat heavily in her special chair. "I can't be taking that girl out with me no more. Those store folk thought I was taking care of somebody's white child." Of them all, my grandmother seemed genuinely to dislike me; I mostly ignored her existence.

The accident of being born with white-appearing features was an invitation for my mother, in particular, to pour into me as much "whiteness" (or her definition of it) as possible. This campaign included speech, ballet and music lessons, classical music, and, definitely, no books by or about black people. Her love of blues and jazz constituted my only exposure to black music, with the exception of spirituals. Unfortunately, that exposure did not translate into a sense of rhythm or dancing ability.

My so-called assets made all the boys in elementary school want me as their girlfriend. It had its effect on teachers as well. Mrs. Carson, my third-grade teacher, selected me to play Snow White in the class play though other girls were more talented. I still have the photograph of light me surrounded by a cast of dark children. Their eyes were all directed toward me, yet, their faces did not show the happiness one would expect from kids who had delivered a successful performance.

Long, thick, wavy hair added to the desired look, but this "almost good" hair was not enough for my mother. Beginning in junior high school, I submitted to weekly hot combs to eliminate thickness and curls. Later, chemical straighteners would achieve the desired result—long, bone-straight, lifeless hair. Like many black women, I carried on a love/hate relationship with my hair into adulthood. At college, when Black became beautiful, I reverted to natural hair and took the bold step of cutting an inch. That unlocked something in me, and as a working woman, I finally got it to just above the shoulders and alternated between natural and straight, depending on my environment and my level of insecurity. Upon a revisit to Hopkinsville, after more than thirty years, among the most consistent comments I got from family and friends was, "oh, you cut off all that beautiful, long hair." The consensus seemed firmly set that among Hoptowners, "blow" hair was still envied. Now, I have convenient hair, in and out of the shower, and that's it. Nothing that takes significant time. I figure if I need some straight hair, I can easily buy it!

Anyway, back to light skin and colorism. I must say, it worked for me in those early days of integration. Teachers assumed I had smarts, and kids and adults alike seemed easy around me. Part of it was color, but the rest, I believe, was speech. I sounded white but without the Kentucky accent. It set me apart from both white and black kids. I learned to become comfortable with my isolation. I envied the children who seemed the perfect definition of assuredness. With minimal effort, it seemed, some kids—both black and white--were able to belong comfortably in any group or situation.

Thankfully, the world has changed drastically over the decades: beauty is found and appreciated in all skin colors and hair textures. Of course, troglodytes remain among us as an increasingly vocal group. I rejoice in this evolution and; though still wanting in assuredness, I have worked hard to dispel and shatter the myths of the past.

# 10: Two More Hopkinsville Memories

I am contemplating my eventual return to Kentucky, and three memories emerge.

### *The first memory:*

Attorney McHenry carried his role as a civil rights crusader even after his death. His last civil rights victory was to be buried in the white cemetery. Oh, the buzz that went through town! Whites were so used to just not seeing black folk at all back then that they talked about anything in front of us—that's how black folk ended up knowing so much about their intentions. The whites just never seemed to get it.

Anyway, plans circulated in the white community to blow up Mr. McHenry's grave to let everyone know their place. There were no cellphones then, but word passed quickly throughout the black community. Without any big discussions or meetings, older black men just appeared at the gravesite with their shotguns. They never protested, and they never said anything. They just stood around drinking their coffee (or other stuff) and shouldering their guns. Some church ladies brought out folding chairs and food. A rotating small three- or four-man contingent stood guard at the grave for more than a month. Nothing happened, and white people's anger—and their nerve—just dissipated. The issue died, and the cemetery was quietly integrated.

***The second memory:***

This is about people who were "musical" (our old-fashioned term for gay) people in our community and their relationship with the kids. The characters are:

AC: gay man; very light skin; successful and monied; funeral-home owner; had a rental property and a couple of nightclubs, where B.B. King and Little Richard often played (This used to be called the "chitlin' circuit.). My mother, Margaret, was sometimes his beard, who served as his public companion—although she was the only one who didn't seem to know it. At one time, she even tried to convince both him and me that I was his kid—even though I already knew and had a relationship with my real father. Many years later, she told me she had planned to marry AC—this despite his all-but-married relationship with another man, Mike.

Mike: AC's longtime lover. Mike was quite effeminate and wore lots of flowing things, sort of like kimonos. He wore his hair "conked," had a gold tooth, and was from New Jersey. He kept the house and helped out with all of AC's businesses.

Charlie (born "Charlotte"): an old-time lesbian—"bull daggers" was what we called them outside their hearing—but she didn't seem to mind the word dyke. In truth, no one called her anything except Charlie. She drove a cab and was one of the few cabbies brave enough to pick up drunken soldiers from clubs in the wee hours and ferry them back to

Fort Campbell. Her girlfriend Jo-Jo was more feminine but still had a "don't mess with me" air about her.

Here's the weird stuff (especially in light of the rise later of homophobia): Nobody, including parents, seemed to mind that we kids hung around these folk. No one explained anything to use, but we could observe and figure out what was what (or maybe who was what). It just didn't seem to matter. In fact, AC adopted a young boy (not for sex, but as a son) when I was in 10th grade. Anyway, often we kids who had gotten permission to go out (that was hard to do for a lot of us) ended up at AC's house, which was quite lavish. Mike would feed us and talk to the boys about how a gentleman behaves and to us girls, about how to carry ourselves like ladies, especially after we had gotten our "womanlies." Of course, we didn't know what he meant—the damned man should have just said "periods." But we listened to him, and he told us stories of being in pageants and living in "mother houses" in New Jersey. Charlie would arrive later and sometimes bring what I guess would be called "rough trade." At first, we were scared of them, but it soon was apparent that they really liked talking with us. To this day, I don't know why. I remember seeing Little Richard at the house; he came there to stay after performing at AC's nightclub. (Few hotels were available to black folk at that time—even to stars.) And I remember Mike admonishing him to watch his language around us.

The other part of this memory was the acceptance that these folk enjoyed in the black community (and among some whites). They were integral parts of the community, and our parents trusted them with us—unlike a lot of the hysteria today. Was it because everyone knew their families or what? Did people just have a clearer picture of these folks as real persons? All the God-fearing black folk just seemed to think of them as one of us—belonging. I think whites just left them alone because they lived and loved within the black community and because of AC's wealth. I'm sure that jokes were made privately, but mostly I never remembered any fear or labeling them as "other"—even though they never made any secret about who they were.

# 11: Transitions

By the time I graduated in 1969, bigger things occupied my mind—and that of the nation. The Beatles had invaded America; young men were being drafted to Vietnam; hippies, peaceniks, and Woodstock happened; women's lib was emerging; black had become beautiful, and Neil Armstrong was poised to take his "giant leap for mankind." I couldn't wait to leave Hopkinsville and join this dynamic new universe.

Despite the distorted world of those first days of integration, many black Hoptowners went on to distinguish themselves. Linda and I became lawyers, fighting for civil rights. Another friend, Gloria Jean Watkins, became "bell hooks," a noted writer and cultural theorist. Our group also included two Rhodes scholars who became leaders in their respective fields. Numerous others earned reputations as professionals, scholars, and businesspeople. The novelty of integration wore off at about the same time the vitality of our town began to fade. Nowadays, few kids of any race manage to go on to achieve their dreams. The promising ones leave.

# 12: After Hopkinsville: Six Years in Twilight

It should be a capital offense for parents to let their children leave home as ignorant and unprepared as I was when I headed off to college. To put it mildly, a bag of hair was smarter, more worldly, and more aware than I was. It is probably lucky for me that I attended a relatively small state college not far from my home. My original choice was McGill University in Montreal, then Canada's top-ranked school; my second choice was Swarthmore College, a private liberal arts school not far from Philadelphia. Swarthmore was not co-ed at that time, which gave me a bit of relief that I would not have to deal with two "foreign" things at once—living away from home and interacting with boys—neither of which I had ever experienced (beyond my summers in St. Louis, which I spent in the company of my cousin's boyfriends and her male cousins). Margaret did not want me to go away—a surprise since she never really acknowledged me while I lived with her in the first place. Anyway, she raged and tormented me about McGill: "You don't know *what* those people are like up in Canada," she'd say. "There's no way I could get to you if you need me." The latter was quite funny since she never had "gotten" to me during the first 17 years of my life when I actually might have needed her. In hindsight, I know she was afraid for me and even more afraid of being alone, despite having a husband and despite the fact that I had last lived with her only during my three years of high school after having spent eight years with my great aunt and uncle.

I got accepted to McGill, but by that time, I had been so battered that I did not reply. And as far as I knew, I'd never even heard from Swarthmore. [But there's a denouement: after Margaret died and I was cleaning out her house, I found a letter addressed to me from Swarthmore; it seems that I had been accepted there as well.] Anyway, left with the alternative of going to the local community college and living at home, I hurriedly applied in secret to Murray State University (MSU), located about 70 miles from Hopkinsville. I knew little about the school other than that it was away from Hopkinsville. I got accepted and got financial aid. Margaret said nothing when I told her I was leaving.

I knew nothing about the college or the town. I knew nothing about living with peers. I had no experience making my own decisions. But I did know that the world was changing and that youth in America was driving that change. I longed to be part of that. I wanted to experiment with different ways of living. I wanted to sit up until the wee hours, talking about life and deep things. I already had done all of this, but only in my mind.

Well, Murray State certainly was different. Calloway County, where the university was located, was a "dry" county—meaning that it banned the selling of alcohol. As a result, I saw more people drinking and drunk during my tenure at MSU than I think I would ever have seen in a place like New York. Students constantly risked life and limb fast—driving the 25 miles on an irregular and unlit road across the Tennessee border, where they got totally smashed and bought liquor to bring back. Frat boys had regular wipeouts along that route. Bootleggers (who were in the business of re-selling rather than making alcohol), moonshiners; marijuana growers; and preachers ruled the county's power structure. Each year the question of whether the county should go "wet" came up on the ballot, only to be defeated due largely to the united efforts of bootleggers and preachers.

The majority of students were from Kentucky—usually from small farming communities, but a few were from Louisville, Lexington, or smaller urban areas. There seemed to be only about fifty or sixty black students that first year. The mix was rounded out by around ten to fifteen Jews; a few New Yorkers and Philadelphians; several Iranians (fleeing the Shah); and Africans. Catholics also were part of the exotica.

Black students were the first to reach out to me, and I tried hard to reach back. But I had little interest in their weekly card parties, dances, and dorm-room gab-fests. I didn't dress or talk like them, didn't know the dances, didn't know the hip sayings. Also, they were laser-focused on education and career. I, on the other hand, was all over the place just trying to experience life free from constraint. Where black students wanted only to interact with each other, I wanted to touch as many different kinds of people as possible and finally be part of that thing that was being called the youth culture.

Finding that youth movement–counterculture world I'd been reading about and seeing on television was a daunting task, and MSU certainly was no Columbia or Berkeley. I knew that on my second day on campus. If the air of change existed at all, it was concentrated in small spaces. Finding those spaces would take some work.

I found one unlikely place—the UCM (or United Campus Ministry) center for students. It was not a place I would normally enter. But I started following a long-haired artist-looking guy on one of my exploratory walks, and I followed him right to the UCM. I stood on the sidewalk for a while and, during that time, saw other "non-regulation" students go in, so in I went. It was the first time that I was the one to make the first move to connect socially. I walked in and was immediately welcomed by Fred, the director, who dressed "straight" but was young and outgoing. Surprisingly, he said nothing about God or religion. He just welcomed me to relax, enjoy television, get a snack from the machines. He introduced me to the person who I soon learned really ran the place—his secretary, June. She was smart, both mentally and fashion-wise. She dressed and looked like "Big City."

That first time, I just sat in the big comfortable chairs and watched whatever came on television. Some other students were doing the same. Others were talking about different events, classes, and professors. About an hour later, a tall, lanky blonde came in and took the seat next to me. We introduced ourselves. She was Carol from Danville, a town in the northeastern part of Kentucky. She was dressed in regulation hippy—a tie-dye T-shirt, jeans, dangling earrings, and granny glasses. It was her first time away from home too. We easily fell into conversation, and when she said, "Let's get something to eat," I said, "Sure." And I'd made my first friend. How easy!

Naturally, I found my fit with the artists and others called "freaks"—those who did not look, think, or act in the conventional mode. They looked disheveled and wore jeans and tie-dye or music- or political- or art-themed T-shirts, had long hair, used drugs, read philosophy, and were open to people who were different. Those stupid-looking Birkenstocks also were a fave for some, although most in our area opted for boots and tennis shoes. Large over-the-top afros were *de rigueur* for those who could achieve it. (I soon learned how much work went into getting and keeping an afro. I was perturbed when some Jewish kids seemed to just "fro" naturally with hardly any effort.)

For the first time, I was able to relax, breathe, and just be who I was or figure out who I was trying to become. The cost, unfortunately, was the few friendships I had with black students, who were bound by rigid rules of convention and peer pressure. They couldn't accept that I was "crossing the line"—mixing so freely with whites, Jews, foreign students, and other "different" beings. Still, it was a small price to pay for the freedom to explore the wider world.

It was no surprise that I landed on academic probation at the end of my first semester. After that, I did only enough work to stay off probation—which was required in order to maintain my student loan and remain eligible for the work-study program. In those plush economic times, it was pretty easy to live on a meager loan combined with work-study. It didn't feel like hardship, since most of us were in the same economic boat. Sure, there were those in my circle who were wealthy by comparison. They had cars, nice apartments, and a regular allowance from parents or some survivor benefits. A few were Viet Nam veterans, supported by the G.I. Bill.

The other thing about that time was that a lot of socializing occurred in groups. That really took the pressure off since I was pretty insecure and terrified about boy-girl interactions. Sex, however, was free and easy. In January 1971, my future husband, Bill, enrolled at MSU as an art history major. He quickly became part of the UCM art crowd. According to Bill, it was May of that year that he decided that I would be his. From that point on, we played a sort of cat-and-mouse game, all the while knowing we were meant for each other. It took until 1975, when I (finally) graduated, for us to "seal the deal"—not by sex, but by his moving to D.C. to be with me.

Thanks to my constantly wearing Dr. Scholl's sandals, my legs had developed to the point that I could survive group outings to the nearby Land Between the Lakes camping and wildlife area. A group of us often would take off for hikes and just sit around enjoying the outdoors. When I first went there, the area had American bison. That soon ended when the Park Service discovered that buffalo could swim. Who would have thought that about a plains animal? Some of them had the habit of swimming across the narrow part of one of the smaller lakes and visiting residents in the adjacent town. So, eventually, it was goodbye, buffalo. But I do remember the awe that they inspired in me getting to see them so dangerously close up. (They always seemed placid and ignored us, but years later, Animal Planet's Planet Zoo TV program showed me the dark side of these beasts.)

I knew there was more to discovering life than sex, drugs, and rock-and-roll, but I didn't know what else there was, so I let myself be swept away, willingly going along with other people's agendas. Dropping LSD or doing other mind-altering drugs was just a regular part of life— something to be shared with friends or for a special event like a concert. At the mention of a concert, a friend and I would hitchhike to other states or across the country. My own plans did not matter enough to me to refuse. Visits to communes like The Farm & Coast Market in Padanaram Village were frequent.

A small hiccup happened when Carol and I got busted for smoking a joint on the street. We ended up "incarcerated" at the sheriff's house, and when we got to court, nobody could figure out how to spell marijuana. Truth. But it was my friend Gary who had the distinction of being the first student to be expelled from MSU because he was caught smoking pot. Of course, my little group of freaks had nothing on the athletes and frat boys who regularly stayed in a mostly alcohol-fueled stupor, usually accompanied by extreme acting-out and violence. It was par for the course for freaks or mixed-race groups to anticipate harassment from a carload of frats and to be prepared to dodge the occasional thrown beer bottle. Amazingly, no one in my crowd became hooked on alcohol or anything else. Almost everyone finished school (eventually) and took his or her place in mainstream society. Those Twilight Years, as I sometimes call them, were like a vast exploratory anything-goes interlude from which we emerged barely scathed. (I feel sad for kids today who can't experience that freedom. Drugs and sex are too-often death sentences, and the economy no longer has the capacity or will to indulge in play.)

For me, the important part of those years was the ability to feed my mind and imagination. It was difficult, but not impossible to plug into what was taking place across the country—and, in truth, with the youth movement around the world. Since there was no black political movement nearby, I embraced feminism, which was emerging on campus and as a global movement. I joined the required consciousness-raising group, where I learned to perceive the world through the lens of feminist analysis. I joined the body-consciousness group, where we read and discussed chapters from the newly-published "Our Bodies, Ourselves"—a sort of ownership manual for women's bodies. A few of my friends gravitated to the Simplicity, Organic, and Back-to-the-Earth track, carrying around and trying out recommendations from the *Whole Earth Catalog* and *The Tassajara Bread Book* and studying midwifery. Others became enamored of explorations in mysticism and spirituality. Still, others began devouring authors such as Ayn Rand, Anais Nin, Emma Goldman, and, of course, the books *The Lord of the Rings* and *Dune*. As I said, it was a time of exploration for everyone—including a number of our professors, particularly those in the art, psychology, and sociology departments. I partook of it all, slipping easily from one group to the other.

One of the pivotal events, while I was in college, was the availability of birth control pills for unmarried women and the limited availability of abortion. (It would not be until 1973 when the Supreme Court issued its groundbreaking ruling in *Roe v. Wade* that made abortions widely and easily available nationwide.) I had already started myself on The Pill (stolen from my uncle's pharmacy) before leaving for college. Curing myself of my virginal state was one of the first things on my to-do list when I got to school. I later worked with a group of women who counseled other co-eds who were experiencing a "problem" pregnancy. The problem in nearly all cases was that they didn't want to be pregnant. Our group talked to the women about options, but in reality, they came to us for only one—where to get an abortion. In those days, we arranged for women to go to New York, which was then the mecca for easy access. This predicament and need was the one unifying thing among women in a college community that was otherwise stratified by race, income, and geographic area of origin. It was women making painful and important decisions and taking control of their futures. Our college ferociously fought against the changing times. One of the few causes that rallied many students on campus was the school's decision to expel a student because she was pregnant and unmarried. Boy, how things have changed.

It would not take long before I had the opportunity to learn that The Pill was not infallible. I did not have to go to New York. I was cured by an understanding and courageous doctor in Tennessee. It certainly was a scare. I could just see my life being over and having nowhere to go. Margaret already had told her friends that I would not be allowed home if I became pregnant. I believed her. I decided to make sure that this wouldn't happen again by having an IUD (intrauterine device) installed. Problem solved, huh? Not true. Later, when I was living in the Pocono Mountains of Pennsylvania, I became pregnant again. Yes, even with the IUD. I spontaneously aborted without much ill after-effect. I was one of many thousand women who were victims of the brand of IUD called the Dalkon Shield. I did not join the class-action lawsuit against the manufacturer, but I am glad that others did. When I returned to Murray State in 1973, I decided to take care of the problem once and for all. I made the rash and too-young decision to get a tubal ligation – permanently eliminating any possibility of pregnancy. I guess I had absorbed a bit too much of Margaret's rantings that having a child was the "worst thing that could happen to a woman." I wanted to make sure that that "worst thing" couldn't happen to me. In my 30s, when other friends had children, I momentarily regretted my decision. I felt it would be good to have a child and give her all the love and nurturing that I never had. Bill and I talked intermittently about adoption, but we never had the determination to plow through the paperwork and process. As a result, we do not have adult children to whom we can become a burden.

Low-cost flights and Eurorail and student hostels made backpacking through Europe one of my required itinerary items. With only a few exceptions, I did all this without having to disclose to Margaret that I was traveling and, in at least one instance, that I had dropped out of school for a semester. It was funny, though, on a couple of occasions, I brought a group of friends home, and my dread was not realized! She laughed and interacted and just seemed like a young, hip parent. It was something that I had never experienced in my life. Those days were too hectic for me to get the backlash that would usually result from such folly.

Then, it all came crashing into focus—my goal and purpose. I had only recently returned (actually, February 14, 1973) to Murray State and Bill from a stint living in Bloomsburg, Pennsylvania, and I was still meandering through life. But, on May 17 of that year, the Watergate hearings opened. Like most of the country, my little group gathered at the United Campus Ministry center to watch "tricky Dick" finally get his due. During those hearings, one majestic, brilliant, patriotic, and healing voice seemed to be speaking just to me. Barbara Jordan, the congresswoman from Texas, questioned witnesses with such authority and knowledge as I'd never seen before from a black woman. The congresswoman expressed a deep and abiding love for our country and righteously demanded integrity from its leaders. Each time she spoke, her deep, resonant voice reminded us of the gravity of the proceedings. To me, she was civil rights, morality, feminism, political honesty, and truth all rolled into one. It was like lightning had struck. *Yes!* I needed to emulate this being. I needed to be a contributor to making this country great—not through its ability to make war on other countries but through its adherence to the ideals of right and fairness.

Acting on this epiphany, I re-enrolled in college, determined to finish my degree and go to law school. With this new determination, I finished up my four-year degree in a little more than two years. I took the Law School Admission Test (LSAT) and applied to several law schools. I wanted to go to one that was an activist and would prepare me to practice law from Day One after graduation. My first choice was Yale because of its strong student clinic in which students provided legal services to indigent clients. Second choice: Antioch, a new all-clinical law school headed by Jean and Edgar Cahn, leading political thinkers and law-setters. Third choice: Harvard—just *because*.

Well, the results: I didn't get into Yale. I went to Harvard for an interview and to meet members of the Black American Law Students Association (BALSA. In 1983, the name was changed to National Black Law Students Association.). I didn't like them, but I got to meet Susan, who was also there for an interview and who also eventually chose Antioch. I got accepted by Antioch. There was no decision to make.

Antioch was the right kind of school, and it was in the right place—the nation's capital. I would be right there near Congress, the president, and the Supreme Court.

With my future in hand, I searched desperately for the right financial package—which I ultimately got. I needed Bill to come with me. He had once said he would follow me "at the drop of a hat." So, with my Antioch acceptance letter, I went to his apartment. When he opened the door, I started tossing hats inside—about 12 in all. He grimaced because he knew what it meant—we were leaving Kentucky. He just didn't know that it also meant that we'd be moving to Washington. After graduating in December, I took a job in Hopkinsville to save up money until I left for Antioch in August.

My seven years of wandering had come to an end. I was able to throw off the shackles of someone else's dream and grab my own. It was twilight no more.

# 13: First Stop in the Promised Land: Chocolate City

In August 1976, I arrived at what would be my home for the next forty or so years. I came to Washington to have my say with our country. But first, I had to get through law school.

Antioch was unlike any other school in the country at that time—I think it still is. It was unabashedly biased, reflecting a liberal, often-radical, activist outlook in nearly every aspect. It prided itself on selecting nontraditional students—those with a demonstrated commitment to the causes affecting poor, disenfranchised, and marginalized peoples. I had that credential in my mind and only limited actual experience, but I got in.

The first rite of passage for all Antioch students was the "live-in." This was a two-week period (my memory is fuzzy here, so it might have been four weeks) in which students lived with a local family. The family was invariably low-income, African American, and living in some of Washington's poorest, most crime-ridden neighborhoods. The school wanted everyone to know first-hand the reality of the lives of the people we would be serving in the clinical program.

The second rite of passage was Professional Methods (PM-I, PM-II, and PM-III), taught by the famous William P.

Statsky, who was a leading authority on legal research and analysis and on statutory interpretation. We were immersed in research, analysis, the art of argument, creating—and finding support for—new legal theories and ethics. We drafted complaints, pleadings, and briefs. We spent countless hours observing court and talking afterward with the lawyers on both sides. We even got to talk with defendants and plaintiffs. We learned how to research the companies and organizations and political leaders that held power. Moreover, our learning and exploration were not confined to the local arena. We took our "classroom" to Capitol Hill, the Executive Branch, federal agencies, the Supreme Court, federal court, and Embassy Row. We met with coalitions and political groups.

Many of the cases accepted by the clinics turned into legal precedents; a few went as far as the Supreme Court. Usually, in those cases, a third-year student teamed (served as co-counsel) with a lead attorney. Often, a group of students would be called to write an *amicus* or "friend of the court" brief. These were heady times; so many new laws were still being made. We carried out our clinical real law practice duties while carrying a traditional law school load. Antioch used a pass-fail grading system—a bit disingenuous since instructors used an internal system to fail you if you did C-level work.

My Waterloo came in the prisoners' rights clinic taught by an ex-con who had become a lawyer. My assignment was to represent prisoners in disciplinary hearings at the Lorton Reformatory, the District of Columbia's prison. If a prisoner lost a hearing, it could mean doing additional time; suspension of privileges such as family visits, library or training time, or work details; removal of trustee status; or even time in isolation. So this was a big deal. Important work—right? The problem was that I was overwhelmed and unnerved by being searched and locked in. (I've always been terrified of being or feeling "trapped.") Also, I just didn't like these guys; I especially didn't want to represent convicted rapists. I didn't know anything about prison culture and how everyone had some kind of game to play. In this setting, it was difficult for me to hold onto the Antioch values that said everyone had a right to representation without consideration of guilt or innocence. Indeed, some of my clients were people I felt should be locked away forever. These days, there would have been some sort of orientation to prison life to prepare and cushion students. Not for us. I think the faculty figured that we didn't need it because of our political beliefs. I got through it, but it was hard. A lot of Antioch was like that—jump right in, sink or swim.

My distress helped me learn one of the key principles of activist practice. The American legal system is founded on the principle that despite the guilt, innocence, or dislike of the person, that person has the right to expect—and lawyers have an obligation to provide—the best, most zealous representation possible. I had to learn that lesson many times over the years. It explains why I can look kindly and empathize when I see lawyers representing the most despicable people—people who I feel do not belong in society. To me, these lawyers are making sure that the legal system works. This is not to say that I don't support reforms, but the right of defendants to be competently represented remains an absolute for me.

One of my law school highlights was serving as editor of *The Abortion Law Reporter*, a legal case reporting and analysis publication by advocates for reproductive freedom. The work was painstaking and exacting and overseen by one of the legends of constitutional law, Burton D. Wechsler. (The man even had the look of William Kunstler.) From him, we learned dedication and reverence for the Constitution, the skills of clarity in legal writing, and the implications of a comma. Funding for the *Reporter* came from the National Abortion Rights Action League (NARAL), and one of our advisors was Ruth Bader Ginsburg, then a professor at George Washington University Law School.

My friends Barbara and Elisa also worked on the *Reporter*. Later we teamed with another friend, Susan, at the Congressional Clearinghouse on Women's Rights, based in the office of Charlie Rose (D-N.C.).There we worked with

Shirley Chisolm, Bella Abzug, and other civil rights leaders to get gender and race equity into legislation. Susan went on to work at a private detective agency in Chicago, where she later was instrumental in the capture of the Unabomber.

The people in my Antioch group of friends were different and quirky. All but one came to law school from careers working on progressive issues. One was very wealthy, but we didn't hold it against her; we only joked about it occasionally. I did feel the second-class citizenship of poverty, though—even at Antioch. It showed up in the fact that I had to work while attending school. It most definitely and painfully came to light when those of us who were poor were unable to accept some of the most lucrative unpaid internships available. These were the internships that launched careers.

But mostly, I didn't let these things bother me. What I remember most about law school was not the classes, cases, courtrooms, study groups, or exams but the tremendous amount of fun we had and the excursions we took. Mostly it was my friend Barbara (now a judge) who was the ringleader and organizer for the fun. She always was the first to hear about a folk festival or exhibit or discover a new nature area. Her enthusiasm was contagious. She would speak, and before you knew it, a whole gang of us would be hunting for someone with a car or van, and we'd be off, not really even caring what it was or where we were going. If we were with

Barb, we knew it would be fun. Drive to New York after a long day in class and at work? No problem. We'd sleep *next* week. My Antioch friendships survive to this day.

# 14: Working for Women in the National Arena

In 1979, I joined the horde of careerist Washington women—tailored suits, Ferragamos, Coach purses, and briefcases. My face took on that Washington woman visage—an "I-mean-business-take-me-seriously" look accompanied by a shoulders-back, purposeful stride. Ready to do battle for the good of the country. And "the good of the country" meant making sure that the government "did right" by our constituency—mine being women, particularly women of color. After a stint at the Legal Services Corporation, I landed my dream job: I was hired by Wider Opportunities for Women, or WOW, to be legislative counsel and finally advanced to become director of the Women's Workforce Network. (WOW's national network of women's employment programs and their supporters.)

WOW was founded in 1964 by two Vassar grads, Jane Fleming and Mary Janney. Both had long histories as activists, especially in the civil rights movement, and they created WOW to push for women's economic and employment success. With influential backing from high-up connections, WOW set out to lead the nation in developing training for women to enter so-called nontraditional occupations, such as skilled construction, mechanical engineering, and other jobs previously considered to be for men only. For the first time, I saw women routinely wearing hard-hats and working confidently. WOW's leaders faced down employers as well as unions to put women on the job. Through its activism, WOW soon developed a network of supporters made up of women's employment organizations, policymakers, funders, and others located around the country. This, in turn, became the Women's Workforce Network, or WWF. WOW also worked closely with one of the early organizations to champion the cause of the "displaced homemaker"—women who were victims of an old story in which a husband leaves his wife of many years for a younger woman or to pursue his own dreams. Up to that time, the wife's job had been confined mostly to the home. Such women may or may not have gone to college, they had hardly any outside work history, and many were ill-equipped to live independent lives, having left major decisions (and their finances) in the hands of their husbands, who had been the family breadwinners. Interestingly, you could count Senator Edward M. Kennedy (D-Mass.), a leading liberal, and Senator Orrin G. Hatch (R-Utah), a prominent conservative, as advocates for this group of women. Compromise and coalition-building were more common then.

Whenever there were meetings, it was almost a given that I would be the only person of color in the room. I set out in search of women who looked like me and soon found women of color hidden away in a number of women's organizations. They were doing important work, but they were not very visible. We came from different backgrounds, had different educational backgrounds, and held different interests and perspectives, but at the core, we were all committed to tearing down obstacles to equality. Without having to discuss it, we quickly began functioning as a women-of-color group within the larger women's community.

Much of the time, we were just there for one another—to provide moral support and boost each others' morale, and to have a safe place to talk about all the anti-progressive, racist crap rolling over us from white so-called feminist leaders. Many of these leaders couldn't accept that despite being feminists, they could also be racist. Some just wanted so much for women of color to be just like them that they tuned out any differences (the old color-blind dodge). My little group tried to be a bridge between the women's rights and civil rights communities. On the surface, we all gave a good public face, but the day-to-day reality was quite different—and complex. In truth, many of our colleagues were well-intentioned but simply oblivious. Others were outright racist while spouting politically correct mantra. We learned to tell the difference. We also had to figure out how to deal with a lot of denial, particularly among our Jewish colleagues, who seem to have staked an exclusive claim on suffering. For many, the blinders never came off, and frank discussions never took place, no matter how much we wanted it. The response was similar to the one exhibited later when we dared pose mild questions about Israeli policies or actions. The conclusion: if you were Jewish, you couldn't be racist, and anyone who raised a question about Israel was an anti-semite. The doors just shut, and discourse fled.

Mostly, we worked together to give a collective tug on the petticoats of these leaders, keeping them from making ill-considered blunders. Actually, that was a lot of what we did. ("No, E., you may not want to say that." "J., "Don't you think it would be a good idea to get the input of the NAACP Legal Defense Fund?" "Yes, M.G., that sounds good, but the impact on people of color would be . . .") The other important thing we did was to try to find leadership opportunities and ways to get each other recognized by groups that were important, but were not necessarily part of the feminist inner circle. We had all grown up being taught that recognition and reward flowed from hard work, but that wasn't true. In reality, recognition flowed from actual or perceived power. Our effectiveness—and the respect we could command at our organizations—depended on our ability to demonstrate that we had our own constituents who valued us. It was the old nobody-treasures-you-until-someone-else-does maxim. Or, in the sexist vernacular, wives are always invisible and taken for granted until some other man shows an interest. Well, we spent time finding and cultivating that other man.

We also supported each other in our personal lives, like holding hands and giving shoulders to cry on at the failure of one more try at in vitro fertilization—and celebrating with abandon when a baby was born. Accompanying each other to doctors' appointments so we wouldn't be alone to hear test results. Encouraging side-ventures and even doing a bit of matchmaking.

With the election of Ronald Reagan, we decided we had to do something different and proclaim ourselves—or at least spout the new rhetoric—while the white girls were trampling over each other trying to fit into the new world order. We knew that it was up to us to make sure that women of color were not left out of the conversation. Meeting secretly after work, we came together to form the Women of Color Access Project. Our goal was to work with women of color to help them build the political résumés that they needed to contend for party positions and political appointments as well as jobs in Congress. I had sat on President Carter's Council on Women's Appointments, and most women of color came before us highly credentialed with many professional accolades. But they were neophytes when it came to the political arena and putting together the political credentials needed to survive the appointment process. The Access Project wanted to get women of color thinking strategically and politically. We got a small grant from the Edna McConnell Clark Foundation to pursue our goals and used Pablo Eisenberg's Center for Community Change as our feed-through organization since we did not have nonprofit status. To keep the organization "in the family" and to show that we were non-partisan, we drew straws over the potluck to see who would become the group's Republican. I won—or lost, depending on your perspective. (Disgusted with both parties, I remained a Republican through a Clinton appointment and until the Obama election. It was easier until recently to focus on issues instead of party labels and to work on both sides of the aisle. By then, I was pretty well known by the leadership of both parties, so my party label mattered less. Besides, I was known to take on either party with gusto, depending on the issue.)

Black women Republicans were scarcer than rare, and I was soon invited to be on all kinds of committees, attend briefings, and meet all manner of people, including the Reagans (and later the Bushes). It was an eye-opener for me as well as the rest of our group. We got to see up close (or as closely as we could) how the private sector operated and got its agenda across. Before that, we had been used to the somewhat messy and clumsy efforts of the Democratic National Committee and the Democratic machine. Now, with the Access Project, we were clearly on a par with our employer organizations, demanding our own seat at the table independent of them. The leaders of our organizations were angry and felt betrayed by us, but they couldn't say a word about it, and they had to sign on in support of our goals and principles. Boy, did we get the glares at work! In addition to the political arena, we also tried to expand our presence among the all-powerful program officers in the big foundations. We didn't change the world, but we did get our toe in the door and held it open for a bit.

I spent seven exciting years at WOW and working with Access Project colleagues. But during my last years at WOW, something bad was happening to me, and I feared terribly that I would not be up to the type of work I had been doing. When I resigned from WOW in 1985, my friends came to help me pack up my desk and were among the first to help me find consulting gigs later. They stood with me and celebrated when I was sworn in to practice before the Supreme Court. I stood with them to support their nominations, their promotions, their adoptions, their periods of angst raising teenagers, their career changes, their re-locations, and now, their retirements. We don't see or hear from each other with the frequency we used to, but we know we are still part of a community. None of us has abandoned the fight for fairness and equity. I am dismayed that decades after WOW, we are fighting the same battle and trying to hold the line against retrenchment. I am heartbroken at the outpouring of downright hostility toward women. Maybe it was always there, but today there is something different. This kind of aberration has gained traction and even approval in some parts of our society.

# 15: Weeds in My Garden

Throughout the early part of my life, I had always thought of my brain as an ever-bountiful garden. Always in bloom. Sometimes capable of interesting confluences and cross-pollination resulting in wonderfully strange hybrids—those were the flashes of brilliance that I was known to get before breakthroughs on any problem. Friends and colleagues counted on it. In my mid-30s, however, all that began to change.

Without warning, weedy tendrils began to sneak into my beautiful garden and multiply like topsy. Because of the environment in which I worked, it was hard at first even to notice that something was wrong. In the late '70s and early '80s, when I started working on or near Capitol Hill, unusual behavior and difficult personalities were simply the norm. There were few restraints on personal "eccentricities" as long as you got the job done when it came to legislation, litigation, and advocacy. A typical Washington week was about 90 hours: in-office work peppered with meetings with constituents, lawmakers, and litigators; then, the "socials"—receptions and "friendly" lunches that were anything but. All were designed to make the wonderful American lawmaking machine work.

No matter what your job, you were expected to work 'round the clock for days if need be when things were "hot"—for example, when your legislation was up for debate or a vote or when your case was being prepared for appellate or Supreme Court review. Nobody asked or cared how you did it. You were expected to call on your own natural capacity and fortitude or to have sense enough to lean on the copious amounts of cocaine, speed, liquor, and other substances that flowed freely through the halls of power.

It was during that time that I discovered my ability to go days without sleep, producing all the while. I would regularly burn out staff members and colleagues who tried to keep up with me. Usually, all it took was an emergency to stave off my descent into a "low" period in which I wanted to retreat from it all. If that wasn't enough, I used whatever was at hand to keep going until the emergency passed. As a senior person in my organization active in coalition-building, I had some control over my schedule, so after the "hot" period, I was able to buy downtime in which to retreat and "veg" out. After all, I had produced copiously just the week before. The needs of the job masked this bounce between "highs" and "lows" to the world, but the problems began to become apparent to me. Sometimes in my "up" periods, I failed to produce at the level I wanted, but I still kept pushing. My down times were sad, however, and provided no rest. I began to question more and more my ability to do the work I loved. I began to think that I had some innate flaw. Maybe I wasn't smart enough to keep up;

maybe I was, at heart, lazy and unambitious; maybe I-don't-know-what.

Soon I was carrying a feeling of worthlessness everywhere without being able to point to a cause. In my eyes, I was useless to anyone or anything. If I had thought clearly, I would have seen that the facts belied this delusion. My personal perspective aside, during this period, I still never missed a meeting or deadline; I continued to lead coalitions, testify before Congress, raise money, oversee projects and staff, work on amicus briefs, lobby, meet and greet at receptions, and do all the other things that were expected of me and more. And I continued to be effective to everyone else. I just couldn't acknowledge it in my own mind.

Things came to a head for me when I had to face a painful decision. I was asked to interview for two plum jobs. I figured that the people who invited me just didn't know the real truth. By the time these two opportunities came along, I had already convinced myself that I was too incompetent to do any meaningful work. And, faced with these two new opportunities, I felt I had to throw in the towel; I cared about the work too much to just be mediocre or just half-there. So I made lame excuses for withdrawing from consideration for both positions. My deepest heart told me that, despite skill and desire, I could not trust myself to always be available emotionally or maintain the energy I'd need to produce in these environments. Both jobs required consistent presence, a high level of functioning, and steady energy and temperament. I would be in the public eye in a new way, and I'd have less control over my schedule. Self-medication would be more difficult. I had thought that I was alone in this affliction, but later I learned that more than half of all Washington organizations were in the habit of accommodating the ups and downs of their "stars." Yet that knowledge came to me too late. My feelings of failure— actually, the fear that I was soon going to fail publicly— loomed over me. The vision of impending disaster grew so strong that, in 1985, I shocked my supervisor and colleagues by abruptly resigning from WOW. As far as I was concerned, my law degree was good only for recycling, and my future career lay somewhere at McDonald's.

Before my world totally collapsed around me, I did try to save myself. About a year or so before leaving WOW, I tried therapy. Most of the white girls I knew were in therapy and had been for a number of years. For a black person, it was unchartered territory. Maybe it was just being southern. Not to denigrate what I'm sure were good intentions by my therapist, months turned into a couple of years during which we slogged through all kinds of dredging up and looking at and talking about. I mean, I had been introspective and analytical from the get-go, as they say. Nothing new was uncovered. No solutions presented themselves. She was all "um-hum," "I see," and "how did that make you feel?" But there were no answers to the problems I was having. I'd bring up the fear of not being able to work, and she'd ask about my childhood! Maybe the problem was that I hadn't totally collapsed and was still producing and working on significant projects as a consultant. So I guess she found it hard to believe me when I raised my concerns. I don't know. It was a constant dance: I'd start off talking about my work anxieties, and before I knew it, she'd have me describing some event from my girlhood.

At the behest of my therapist, I tried a few months of group therapy. It was pretty disastrous. But it moved me from meeting in the darkened office in her house to a light-filled space in her offices near the National Zoo, where I could retreat to a coffee shop immediately afterward. There ought to be a law that requires therapists to have a post-therapy space where you can decompress and reassemble yourself. Anyway, at the first meeting, those girls were already primed, just waiting for a group so they could start confiding and emoting and crying all over the place about what I thought were pretty solvable problems. (My own problems didn't instill empathy for those of others.) I was sort of blown away. We had barely shared our names. I was the only black person in the group I dubbed the Zoo Group, but that was not an unusual situation for me, and I felt comfortable with the women. I think I was just too analytical for group therapy. I wanted to confront—not deeply explore—a problem and find solutions. I was faithful, missing only one meeting (one day when I just couldn't face all the emoting), but I never did take "my turn" at breaking down. I don't think it was necessarily a racial thing, but my upbringing didn't allow me to act out or show emotion— especially about traumatic things. You just accepted that something bad had happened, and you went on with fulfilling your obligations. This had surely helped me survive. Besides, even if I had acted on or shared my feelings, there would have been no one to listen or give me comfort. Certainly, when I was a child, no one asked my opinion about any decision being made about my life. That type of sensitivity is part of modern child-rearing in which children and their positive development are at the center of family life. In my world, children were to be seen and not heard. They did what they were told. All my acting out and emoting took place in my head. The barrage of emotions that poured out from therapy group members overwhelmed me and silenced me. I remained that way—attentive, offering suggestions, yet keeping myself uninvested—throughout the life of the group, which thankfully ended when everyone announced plans to go away for weeks during the summer.

I returned to individual therapy, still hoping that something would happen. I just didn't know anything else. By that time, I had left WOW, an event that never was touched on in therapy despite my lengthy explanation of the trauma of the decision. I guess that since I was still insured under my husband's health plan, there was nothing to talk about and no need for urgency, huh? (That's just me being cynical.) Unconsciously, I knew I had to do something— something to break off this never-ending therapy trip and something to get closer to finding out what was wrong with me and then fixing it. Dealing with the nothingness of my therapy was becoming more stressful than the problem I came to resolve. It would take drastic measures to find the fix.

I was just following along in my rut without giving a thought to trying to find a different kind of therapist or a psychiatrist. It just seemed to take too much effort. Hell, I was still unsure how to even articulate the problem. A stable or more experienced person would have found a new therapist, but by then, I was too beaten down to make rational decisions. I was also a little scared of leaving the devil I knew, my therapist, and "going it alone." Pharmaceuticals never occurred to me as a solution. I knew people who took anti-depressants, but they seemed to be as messed up as they ever were. I didn't know how to look for a psychiatrist. At that time, turning to the internet was not so automatic. Also, I was still trying to get someone to clue me in on what I considered to be my personal character flaw.

By chance, I saw a television show in which a high school girl cut herself as an action to exert control (or something like that). Anyway, that character in the show seemed to be getting actual help from her doctor! She seemed to be getting her life back. I know this was mostly due to the Hollywood writers, but, for some reason, it spoke to me. I thought of it like triage in an emergency room—visible wounds get you seen first.

Anyway, to make a long story short, television informed real life, and the seed of an idea began to take root. Maybe I could do something dramatic like cut myself as a way to shake things up and get put on the right road. I was just that desperate. Now, I didn't want to actually hurt or scar myself. Typical of me, I read a lot and took months for preparation. I found the right knife. I made sure it was very sharp. (I knew it would be worse to be cut by a dull knife—and it also would require more force and intention than I might be able to muster.) Then I spent several more weeks building up to the moment, finally laying the blade on my skin to see how it felt. Then, I had to decide where to cut—a thigh would be best, but I didn't want to have to raise my dress or drop my pants to show the wound. I also didn't want to get blood on my clothes. I opted for the outer arm, very far from any vein. In the summer, when I was wearing short sleeves, I began to make the first invisible scratches—none of which drew blood. I lost my courage. But I got it back the next week and tried again. I used a nano-bit more force and pulled the knife quickly across my flesh. Ah. One little bead of blood. Not enough to take to my therapist. So I made a schedule, timing my practice for when I could concentrate on the task—when Bill was out and when I wasn't busy with something else. After a shower worked well. Finally, success! A thin, not-too-deep, but sure and determined scratch that barely qualified as a cut was finally achieved, and that produced a line of blood. Then it healed nearly invisibly before my next therapy session. Damn! It reminded me of the months it took to lose my virginity in college. I'd have to do this several more times to produce something visible. And I'd have to time it to coincide with therapy. Now, I didn't want anyone to think I was interested in suicide. It was quite the opposite of suicide: I was taking drastic measures—I was shouting in my own way—in an effort to save myself.

So, finally, with persistence, I amassed enough scratches to be visible on very close inspection. With that accomplishment, I almost proudly thrust my arm in front of my therapist at our next session. The usual "un-huh" froze in her mouth as she took a deep breath and said she wanted me to see a psychiatrist. Then, she left the room and called to schedule an appointment for me. I wouldn't go that day but agreed to go the following day. Finally!

As I was getting ready to go to my appointment, another dilemma arose. How was I going to keep the first session with the psychiatrist from being wasted on the cutting (which I had stopped as soon as the appointment was made)? In fact, after accomplishing my purpose, I went about investing in any number of unguents, miracle lotions, stretch-mark reducers, and other things to remove the scratches.

The good thing about going to a therapist who treated upper-middle-class and wealthy clients is that she referred me to the best. My shrink has consistently been named by his fellow doctors as the one they would most recommend to their family and friends. Until this experience, I had the common stereotype about psychiatrists—you know, you lie on a couch and talk for ten years about potty training and everything your mother did wrong. Well, damn it, I had been reviewing this stuff all my life. I was proof that childhood is survivable. The past had already happened; I needed to write my future. I had learned from my therapy experience, and I was willing to "waste" some time—but only a little—before getting some answers. This psychiatrist was on a deadline, whether he knew it or not.

On January 15, 1987, I walked into the office of Dr. John M. Livingood like a cuckolded customer ready to demand an accounting. He was tall, well over six feet. He was clean-shaven; thank goodness there was no Freud-like beard. He looked you in the eye and talked directly, with no artifice. His first question asked for my take on what was going on and what I thought was wrong. Boy, it had been so long since I'd been asked that question. I was ready. He smiled when I unfolded my list, which included dates and behaviors that were troubling. Then, he asked a lot of questions. I didn't mind because I felt he was trying to close in on something elusive, and I was willing to give him a chance. We talked about physical health, and he wrote out instructions for a number of labs. That was refreshing, too. At last, we brought science into the equation. In 1987, Prozac was all the rage. It was being prescribed for every illness, mood change, acne, and distress in pets. So, he gave me a prescription to try to see if it had any positive effect. (It ended up being discarded later by mutual decision.) I couldn't help myself: as I was leaving, I asked if he wanted to talk about the cutting. He nonchalantly replied that he didn't if I didn't. How could I have so lucked out? At our next meeting, he went over the results of my labs and asked more questions about me, my family, and my life. Then, he gave his diagnosis: bipolar disorder—a result of biochemical imbalance and hereditary disposition. There was finally a label. And, it wasn't my fault. I now had an enemy to which I could point—and combat. I was elated!

With a name for what I had, we could finally attack this thing. Little did I know the trial-and-error nature of pharma-psychiatry. My doctor was a leading authority at the forefront of poly-pharmacy—using multiple drugs (in other words, a drug cocktail) to treat mental illness. He went about his work with diligence and patience. The best and most promising drug, lithium, caused too many negative side effects for me to use. So it would take a few years of testing one drug and then discarding it or adding another to it before I would land on the right cocktail of drugs that fit my individual case. Still, in all that time, I felt better and seemed to make more progress than I ever had in all my wasted years of therapy.

With a diagnosis, I began to educate myself about the disease and learned about the different types and gradations of bipolar disorder. Not all of us jump off bridges, kill people, or lose touch with reality. The more I learned, the more alarmed I became when the words "bipolar" seemed to leap from the lips of every newsperson reporting a story about any madman who killed people or shot up or blew up a building or every woman who murdered her family or any person acting in an extremely anti-social manner. The story format was always the same: "So-and-so held 20 people hostage in a McDonald's and died in a shoot-out with police; he was said to be bipolar." I was never a person given to sharing freely about personal matters, but this kind of sensational reporting drove me deep into the closet, fiercely guarding the secret of my condition. Hell, if people knew, they would be afraid to sit next to me lest I pull out an AK-47 or something. The media never seemed to report that there were many gradations of the disease or that people were walking around with it and leading productive lives.

Slowly, over the years, I have become braver about sharing information about my disease with others. I don't push it, but rather I wait until the subject of mental health arises naturally—like when someone dismisses a person's comments or decisions as being attributed to craziness or mental illness or, usually, a bipolar condition. Then I make a casual non-pronouncement that I am bipolar. A lot of people act as though they don't hear me. Others respond dismissively as though I had just said made a clever retort: an understated "oh," and the conversation continues uninterrupted. On the rare occasion, someone will actually ask what this means. Then I talk. Even though it is a complex disease with all shades of difference, you have to be careful about telling someone too much all at once. The trick is to share some information while addressing the person's real question—the one that makes them want to move quickly away and watch you furtively. Mental illness is treated socially like AIDS or cancer was in only the recent past. I've seen some progress, though, as more and more people come forward and get diagnosed and treated—especially people of color who more often have been victims of the medical-care system than beneficiaries. I long for the day when I can tell someone about my problem and have him or her deal with it the same as if I'd admitted to having high blood pressure.

The person may not be interested as a matter of course, but he or she needs to understand that there's no reason to be frightened.

Today there seems to be a new public effort to de-stigmatize mental illness. Although I am sometimes aggravated by celebrities trotting forward claiming the mental illness *du jour*, I guess this is progress. Still, people remain leery and too quick to label and too inclined to assume that mental illness defines the totality of a person.

For decades now, I have operated on an even, productive keel. I miss those wonderful highs, but I know that I pay the price for them with poor judgment and rash decisions and with the subsequent near-crippling lows. Some days on the meds, I walk around feeling like imitation crabmeat—you know, sort of real but not quite. But those times never last more than a few days. I have been so "normal" for so long that I no longer think of bipolar as a personal stigma. Maybe I've just gotten too old to care about others' reactions. I hate the regimen of meds, but I'm thankful for them nonetheless. My biggest fear is that I will be unable to afford the insurance that makes the meds affordable. I do wish I had been rescued early on, and I often wonder what my life would have been, had I been able to follow my original dreams. I sometimes ask myself: why didn't anyone intervene or take me to a doctor? I am sometimes angry at my old friends, who I think should have known something was wrong. And I am fleetingly angry at myself when I think my rescuer should have been Bill, but then I remember that Bill was the one person who totally accepted all my differentness. I chose him as my life partner in part because I knew he'd never try to change me. Still, couldn't some of my more worldly friends have intervened? I guess since I always made deadlines and meetings and met all my other obligations, the thought never occurred to them that I needed help. Maybe they were just unable to identify what was unusual in a place and time where so much was out of the norm? I work to avoid wasting energy on what was, but letting the past go is difficult.

In my low moments, I have a recurring fantasy about who and what I could have been had bipolar disorder not attached itself to me. I see other friends who have achieved their career goals in the political and legal arena and feel a momentary pang of jealousy. But in the next moment, I remember the wonderful, exciting consulting career I've had. I was able to do a lot of different things: lobby Congress on higher education; present a Supreme Court brief; get a White House appointment; investigate discrimination complaints; serve on bar association committees; help test new ways to provide evidence of discrimination in litigation; evaluate mental health court models; consult with universities and foundations on employment and chronic poverty. There was never a dull moment, and if I am honest,

I have to acknowledge that doing a variety of projects appeals best to my personality. That would have been difficult if I had been tied to performing one job in a single organization or following some more traditional career path. So, I guess that even though I have to remain vigilant because the weeds are still lurking around, I am enjoying a lush and fruitful garden. I just have to stop long enough to notice.

# 16: Reinvention

After the bipolar diagnosis and subsequent merry-go-round of psyche drugs, good mental health was a priority in my life. I still needed to earn a living, but I had to structure my work and personal life in a way that would contribute to my mental health. I needed the ability to control my work environment; that meant working mostly from home. Deadlines I could handle. It was the chaos and needless frenzy of the typical office that sent me over the edge. Despite great progress and long periods of stability, I still wasn't totally confident that I could maintain the high levels of energy and long hours required for most of my projects. My mainstay was Jannie, a sister-friend I had met while working at WOW. She had experienced her own breakdown of sorts and dropped out of the national scene.

Jannie and I made a great but somewhat odd pair. She had a communications degree from Simmons, and I was who I was. She grew up in a very oppressive family—even more so than mine—in South Carolina and was the eldest of a slew of siblings to whom she became a mother figure. She "got" me, and I got her, and our relationship, up until she died a few years ago, was based entirely on love. I had known this pure love and acceptance from only two other people—Daddy Ernest and my husband, Bill.

Anyway, in the interest of both our well-being, I set about reinventing myself—from national to local. D.C. is unique in that usually, about half the people who live and work there operate only on the national level and identify with a place outside the city. True, there was a rich tapestry of neighborhoods and regular people who had lived in the capital area for generations, but they were largely invisible to those concerned about so-called bigger issues. I did try to maintain my old relationships, but our lives were just too different now. We no longer saw each other regularly in meetings or strategized around common issues. Although we supported each other in our personal lives, it just wasn't enough. And I just couldn't bring myself to say the word "bipolar" to any of them, so I know (now) that they were confused when I dropped out. We still call each other and do Facebook and send each other best wishes. We also are able to have lunch—after much planning and rescheduling. Still, what happened was that I left that society.

If I was to survive, I'd need to find another group of women to which I could belong. Luckily, leadership programs were cropping up in big cities around the country, and Leadership Greater Washington had started just two years after I left WOW. So, pulling strings and calling in chits, I was accepted into the organization's third class of 1989. In one fell swoop, I was cast in with a diverse group of people from the nonprofit, government, philanthropic, and business worlds, all united by the desire to do what they could for the betterment of the region.

At my first Leadership Greater Washington meeting, I started hunting around for women of color whom I could approach. Most were from nonprofit organizations and had been working for years to help District residents, so they all knew or knew of each other. Still, they weren't stand-offish, and people seemed to get along across sectors and races in this group. At one time in D.C. or the surrounding area, if you saw a race or sector-integrated group, it was a sure bet that those folks were connected to Leadership Washington. We really loved and cared for each other as much as for our community. At the end of our year-long leadership program, our class was dubbed "Boring But Bonded." The women (and some men) I met there became my family and support group. (I still see some of them today.) Through them, I built a new identity. Given that it was D.C., there were times when the national and the local intersected; but I had lost my appetite for that larger arena. Interestingly, it was after leaving the national platform that I received a White House appointment to the U.S. Department of Agriculture to create procedures for them to use in processing discrimination complaints. I did the job, but I believe the agency will was never there. I couldn't stay away from the political, though, and soon found myself knee-deep in the workings of Montgomery County, Maryland. It was one of the nation's wealthiest counties, but there was plenty of work to be done on behalf of women and people of color. I still had to balance my public life with my secret bipolar life. Only Jannie was truly clued in on that. But we did it. I remember her last gift. As I was struggling to write this book, I asked for her thoughts and remembrances. Although she was terminally ill, she made the arduous trip from South Carolina to my home in Maryland just to support me that one last time. This book would not exist without her.

# 17: Aunt Fannie's Funeral

My Aunt Fannie finally won the life-long one-upmanship game played among members of my mother's family. Unfortunately, she was unable to enjoy it. For three days, I watched it, locked in a snow globe of sights, sites, and events that rendered me amazed and speechless. I held my breath through it all.

It all started with a Tuesday late-night February phone call from Margaret, my mother. My Aunt Fannie, her youngest sister, was dead at 70. Growing up, I had spent summers with them, enjoying a brief period of normalcy in what was my otherwise chaotic home environment. There was my Aunt Fannie, her husband, Uncle Richard, my cousin Diane, who bore an uncanny resemblance to my mother, and their dog, Alfie—a present to my uncle from the producers of the movie by the same name. (He and his jazz group, the *Quartette Trés Bien*, had worked on the musical arrangements.) Diane, also an only child, was like my sister. We didn't always get along, but we loved each other fiercely. Each day during the summers, we plotted adventures to be played out under the radar of my aunt's vigilance. As Diane moved into her teens, I became the designated "chaperone"—and foil—who enabled her to get out of the house to see boys. A lot of times, we got caught. The family was well-known, and there was always someone to see and report. Punishment was meted out equally, even though I had no real control over where we went or who we saw. I never held it against Diane.

Uncle Richard worked hard, came home, was reasoned and consistent, and enjoyed being with us. His goodness and love for people was evident in all he did. Physically he was a large man, an acclaimed athlete in his youth, and as an adult, he was an avid bowler and golfer, carrying on a lifelong love of sports. He was a true "son of St. Louis," known and beloved widely. His large family took me in as one of their own. While Uncle Richard's world was all of St. Louis and beyond, Aunt Fannie's realm was the home, and she seemed to enjoy it. When she went out with Uncle Richard, her petite frame was always coifed and draped in the latest, most expensive fashions, everything coordinated to enhance her "red bone" coloring. It was many years before I began to understand the difficult burden of her extreme shyness in the face of my uncle's gregariousness. To me, Aunt Fannie was kind and hip and two-faced, but I loved her just the same. She and my mother had a difficult relationship, built on jealousy, love, and genteel competition—the kind that growing up in the South breeds. With Aunt Fannie's death, my mother was the last of her siblings (or so I thought), and I was curious how she would handle the loss.

Anyway, I caught the first flight out from Baltimore-Washington International Airport, and after a few hours of being stranded by snow in Illinois, I arrived in St. Louis late Wednesday.

My Aunt's tastefully appointed house, with its off-limits, plastic-covered living room, was a whirlwind of excitement. Diane was darting around like a deranged wind-up toy rattling off to-do lists, issuing orders, sorting through her mother's closet, whipping in and out of the kitchen, dishing up plates of food, and answering the constantly ringing telephone. I hid in my room and unpacked—way too quickly, Diane and Margaret found me.

Diane skipped the pleasantries and dove right in.

"*The wake is tomorrow evening.*" She paused a beat. "*What did you bring to wear?*" I knew what was coming but responded bravely. "I brought a nice pantsuit for the wake and a dress and jacket for the funeral." I relaxed, proud for once that I had all the bases covered. I should have known better.

"*No hat?*"

"No."

"*No fur?*"

"No."

"*Well, the wake is going to be a jazz dinner party. You'll need evening wear.*"

I didn't respond.

"*Did you at least bring wigs to wear?*"

Again, no response.

*"Well. There's nothing we can do about it,"* she sighed. *"Tomorrow we'll go shopping so you'll be able to properly represent the family. You'll need several outfits to cover all the events."*

"All the events?" What was I signing onto? Diane and her mother loved to do things "big," so I knew I was in for something extravagant. I just didn't know what form it would take. Margaret sat silently on the bed, staring at her folded hands, giving no hint of what was to come.

Early the next morning, before I could even get a cup of coffee or a slice of toast, Margaret, Diane, and I piled into her car and sped to Diane's favorite dress shop, where I tried on several outfits, turning on command like an obedient child for Diane's critique. Margaret echoed the opinions of the sales clerk and Diane, depending on which one had spoken last. We soon settled on a simple teal blue evening gown as well as a backup outfit. (Back-up?) Having averted the evening-wear debacle, we still faced the problem that I might be the only woman present not wearing a mink or fur or hat or elaborate wig. I would be dragged only so far down this road of "correctness," so Diane relented. Given the weather and the travel hardships, she thought I could be "forgiven" any inappropriateness and allowed to wear my own very nice leather coat with fur trim and simply pin up my hair.

Leaving the store, we stopped at the bank to retrieve Aunt Fannie's jewels from the safe deposit box and continued on to the funeral home. Inside the parlor, Diane inspected the mortician's work and turned to ponder which of two couture dresses her mother would wear that evening. I listened as Margaret and Diane discussed color, drape, hairstyles (there were several wigs to choose from), and jewelry. After much back and forth, Diane settled on a satiny, form-fitting red dress with a matching scarf and long gloves. This would be accessorized by a diamond necklace, drop earrings, and an upswept honey-blond wig. The casket would be festooned with a pin that spelled FANNIE in an arc of large rhinestone letters. I was speechless. My experience with funerals was minuscule, but I had never heard of the corpse dressing up for a party. Maybe this was a way of sending her off to eternal festivity in the next life? How Egyptian! The funeral director assured us that everything would be perfect and ready for the wake. Aunt Fannie would arrive at the venue at least thirty minutes before the wake so Diane could conduct her last-minute inspection.

On the way home, Diane explained more of the agenda. The wake; separate events for the ladies and gentlemen; the funeral; interment; and last, a gathering of a few "special" people at the house. Was this some Midwestern thing or St. Louis tradition? I took a big gulp of air, clamped down on any acerbic responses, and squeaked out a comment about the weather. What I really wanted to ask was whether these folk had lost their minds. The comedienne in me wanted to ask whether Aunt Fannie had RSVP'd to these events. As I was to learn later, this actually was a serious question.

At home, Diane gave us a copy of the agenda for Aunt Fannie's *"Homegoing"* (it was the first time I had heard this term):

- Thursday evening: Jazz dinner wake
- Friday morning:
  - Fashion show and brunch for ladies
  - Golf (driving range), cards, and other activities for gentlemen
- Saturday morning:
  - Funeral at church
  - Interment at cemetery
  - Repast
- Saturday early evening:
  - Wine and Cheese
  - Video Viewing

Deadpan (no pun intended), Diane said, "Mother plans to attend all the events except, of course, the men's outing. I'm going to make sure she's the best-dressed in the room." Was it that they just didn't want to let this woman go? I started thinking about Norman Bates and his poor taxidermied mother being moved about the house. In the end, I nodded and made a non-committal sound. I would be doing that a lot.

The jazz dinner went off without a hitch. My uncle's old jazz group played wonderfully, and everybody was in a bon vivant mood. The casket was tilted ever so slightly so Aunt Fannie could oversee the affair like a good hostess. We were afforded a full-body view of her in her brilliant dress and jewels. No one seemed to think anything was odd. I couldn't stop myself from going around to the back of the casket to see. The whole thing was held up by something that looked like an industrial-sized easel. It made me nervous. I expected any minute to be treated to the spectacle of the whole thing slipping and Aunt Fannie being catapulted across the floor. The thought was both horrific and hilarious. I moved far to the other side of the room (just in case) and kept a straight face.

A cocktail and plate of food were placed on a table next to the casket. (In easy reach?) Many guests stopped by the casket to congratulate Aunt Fannie on the party and her outfit. One guy said, "If Richard wasn't so jealous, I'd ask you for a dance." Local as well as nationally known musicians dropped by to sit in on jam sessions or just catch up with old friends. A few white people who had worked with my uncle came by and strolled the perimeter holding onto stiff drinks and smiles. The cool jazz and age-friendly lighting created a dreamlike aura in the hotel room. Tuxedoed men and elegant women mingled, their laughter swirling like tiny shards, brilliant and enervating. It was one of the few times I did not feel awkward in a social setting—especially one with my often-unpredictable family.

By the time it was over, near midnight, we were all exhausted with remembrances and laughter. On the way home, Diane, Margaret, Uncle Richard, and I rehashed the evening. At home, we separated—Diane, Margaret, and me around the dining room table, them with hot chocolate and me with scotch. Uncle Richard went to his now-solitary bedroom, needing nothing but his own thoughts.

The next day, Friday, was the fashion show brunch and the men's morning excursion. Dutifully, Aunt Fannie waited in a place of honor as mimosas and food were served, and thin young women teetered around tables modeling pastel spring wear. To my relief, Aunt Fannie was reclined in the proper position for a dead lady. The beauty of the models and guests was no match for Aunt Fannie, who was once again the star of the event. For this occasion, she wore a couture beaded suit the color of sea foam so rich that it made you want to dive in. Again, her make-up, hair, and jewels were impeccable. The conversation was light, with comments on the wonderful outfit Aunt Fannie had "chosen" for the event. Several people stopped by the casket to compliment Aunt Fannie on her "look." To me, her "look" was "dead," but I concentrated on eating and keeping quiet. Diane kept busy pointing out which of the outfits modeled would look good on her mother. "Mother has just the right figure and coloring to go with that yellow two-piece." I kept a deer-in-the-headlights look on my face and took frequent ladylike sips of my mimosa, wishing it was a single-malt.

We returned to the house, followed a bit later by Uncle Richard and his brother, who reported their event a success. We all sat around the table exchanging family and friends stories, but Diane kept leaving abruptly to make last-minute calls to the funeral home, the church, and various people. Later that afternoon, Diane and I looked at the obituary, which had been left to my mother to prepare. We read the names of strangers. Who were all these siblings and survivors? Surely we must have met or seen these people though we never knew them as kin. Where were they—or their children? Margaret deflected our questions. I guess one of the interesting things about death is family revelations.

On Saturday morning, Margaret, Diane, Uncle Richard, and I piled into the limousine and headed to church for the funeral service. We sat in the first pew and gazed fixedly at Aunt Fannie, who was decked out in a demure white suit and small pearl earrings. People came by to offer condolences and hugs. Now, this more resembled my image of a funeral!

Assistant Pastor Sutton, who was barely a foot taller than the podium, brought us to attention and started the ceremonies. A scriptural reading (Psalm 90 from the Old Testament). A prayer led by one of the deacons. Then a solo, *Precious Lord*. This was the warm-up to welcome the tall, stately senior pastor, Reverend Riley, to the podium. He greeted us stentoriously, *"Our Lord and Savior has called his child home to rest, where every day is Sunday and Sabbath has no end."* From there, he turned to the New Testament (John 14:1-6): *"Let not your heart be troubled . . . . My Father's house has many mansions."* Just as Pastor Riley was hitting his stride, eliciting "yeses" and "amens" at rhythmic intervals, a tinny phone ringtone playing "Strangers in the Night" wafted over the room. Everyone tried to ignore it but couldn't as the song continued to play. People looked around. It was my Aunt Jo's cell phone. She was Uncle Richard's older sister, sitting resplendent in a cream silk number complemented by a hat worthy of the Kentucky Derby. Reverend Riley paused while Aunt Jo took her call. We all listened while she greeted her caller and confirmed their date for a dinner dance that evening. I guess no one wanted the funeral to interfere with the social life of the living. Maybe everyone had just had enough of the social life of the dead by this point. Aunt Jo finished her call, gave Reverend Riley a slight nod, and he continued his sermon. *"I am the Way, the Truth, and the Light . . . ."* He continued to intone until it was time for family to come forward and share personal tributes and reflections. From the immediate family, only Uncle Richard spoke. When he finished, he went to the casket and kissed Aunt Fannie with a very loud "smack" on the lips that echoed through the church. I'm sure I wasn't the only one silently chuckling at this incongruous sound in such a somber setting.

With the choir singing quietly, we took turns making the last goodbye pass in front of the coffin. The family went first, each member stopping to murmur secret words to Aunt Fannie. I didn't have anything to say, but I moved my lips silently as protocol required. I also looked carefully to see if Aunt Fannie might break out in a smile. I think maybe she did, but perhaps it was only my eyes playing a trick. We returned to our pew and watched as the rest of the congregation took their turn on the good-bye walk. Several stopped by our pew to repeat condolences and murmur comments on how beautiful my aunt looked: "just like she's asleep," the perfect ensemble, Diane's good taste, etc.

Finally, the minister gave his parting words, and the choir went into a snappy, praise-Jesus number that signaled the recessional. Aunt Fannie headed the line, we were next, and then the pews emptied one by one as the congregation followed us out of the church for the procession to the cemetery. Aunt Fannie led in the hearse, followed by us in the limo and an endless stream of send-offers. Diane puffed with pride at the number of cars and people honoring "momma."

At the cemetery, the pastor said a prayer while we sat in the damp air, eye-level to the casket. Uncle Richard and Diane each placed a rose on the casket. The machine quietly lowered the casket into the grave. It was over. You don't know how happy and relieved I was to see that woman finally go in the ground! Just when I started to draw my first normal breath since arriving in St. Louis, Diane leaned close to explain that the grave had been dug especially deep so that she, her son, and her father could be buried right on top of Aunt Fannie. All that came out of me was a little exhalation of air that sounded like a feeble "oh."

From the cemetery, we returned to the church for the repast. The church ladies really laid it on—turkey, ham, chicken, greens, and more. I was hungry by this time but couldn't muster the wherewithal to eat. I put a sample of everything on my plate. The family sat on a dais, where everyone could watch us eat. People came by and said comforting words that I forgot as quickly as I forgot the people. I concentrated on keeping my knees together in a ladylike fashion. It was hard. Thankfully, this part of the ritual did not last long, and people expected the family to retire quickly.

Soon, we headed back to the house to change into our "relaxed social" attire and prepare for the final act in this macabre show. The caterers had preceded us and were busy setting up wine and cheese and hors d'oeuvres stations by the time we arrived. Just as we finished getting into our hostess outfits, the special guests arrived, most having changed from their funeral attire. They got drinks, mingled, and talked; they didn't need us. These were close family friends who had visited often and felt at home. A slide show had been set up in one half of the basement-and-game room so people could view pictures from the wake, the fashion show-and-golf event, and the funeral. I walked around holding onto at least four fingers of scotch just to keep my mouth busy. The last slide was of the gravesite and mourners. People actually watched this—including those who had been present at all the events! Several guests filled out little cards to order their own copies of the video. (Huh?) I kept checking my watch, counting down the time until morning, when my plane was scheduled to leave.

As I lay in bed that night, I pressed the rewind and played the old movie reel in my head, and I actually was impressed. I symbolically tipped my hat—the one I should have packed for the homegoing—to Diane. She had pulled it all off, and the "all" was something truly inspired. It was certainly beyond anything that I could have imagined. As Diane and Margaret saw me off at the airport, Margaret pinned me with eyes full of defeat. She just knew that when *she* died, the most I'd be able to muster would probably be an eventless cremation. Fannie had won, once and for all.

# 18: Fatherless No More

I was six years old when I joined the large, silent, and mostly invisible army of fatherless daughters. My mother and father became sweethearts when they were both in the third grade. That love affair lasted through their college years, after which they both returned to their hometown of Hopkinsville. Reunited, they soon had a child, my older sister, who died in her first year of life. Two years later, they had me. Confronted by my mother's repeated refusals to leave her parents' home and join him in starting a new life, my father signed up for a two-year hitch in the Army, hoping that having some time apart would make a difference. It did not. Finally, frustrated, my father met and married another woman and quickly produced two daughters.

I saw my father frequently while I was growing up. Our lives circled each other, visible but never quite touching. When happenstance put us together, we were cordial, but our behaviors never betrayed a more intimate relationship. After a brief hello, we stared frozen-faced, each waiting for the other to make the first move until the moment stretched out too long, and any chance at connection had passed. I didn't know then that I had the power to break through this impasse or that my father was just as confused and unsure as I.

Physically, my sisters, my father, his family, and I bore striking resemblances to one another. Unlike most children of that time who were born outside marriage, I bore my father's name along with his face. There was only one black family named Brooks in our town, so kinship was evident. That did not stop a few adults (and some children) from asking me to name my relations (it's a Southern thing). Most times, these questions were a mean, small-town form of entertainment. Either way, I'd usually just smile and stare mutely at the inquirer until he or she grew uncomfortable and changed the subject.

In his absence, I still carried on with my life. I won piano competitions and essay contests and got A's on my report cards. With every success, I hoped secretly that my father would take notice. Fatherlessness only became truly unbearable on special occasions, like the time our ninth-grade home economics class came up with the foolish and insensitive idea of "Daddy Date Night," where girls invited their fathers to join them at dinner specially prepared by the class and served by the cafeteria workers. For sure, there were other girls sitting next to empty seats at that table, but I barely noticed them over the chasm of my own empty chair. That's when things were very bad.

Over the years, there has been a lot of talk about the impact on boys of the absence of a father, but the impact on girls can be just as devastating. Fathers teach girls about men and give them confidence. Research shows that girls without fathers drop out, make poor choices, engage in anti-social behaviors, and even earn less than girls who have a relationship with a father. Although my mother cited Daddy Ernest as her deepest, most important relationship, she seemed to lack the ability or awareness of my need for a father. Neither Daddy Ernest nor her boyfriends or my stepfather fit the bill. In any case, I both experienced and avoided many of the pitfalls of fatherlessness.

I left my hometown right after graduating high school. I went to college and law school, settled into a career, and married a good man. Still, throughout, I wore the skin of fatherlessness like an old sweater whose scratchiness remains an irritant even though, at times, it is often possible to ignore. It was as simple and as complicated as needing him to know me, accept me, and love me just because I was on earth. I needed to be as important to him as he was to me. It didn't matter that I was an educated, competent professional and victor of many life challenges. It didn't matter that I had a loving and devoted husband. Despite my strong independent woman image, some primitive part of my brain called for the assurance and protection of a father. It didn't matter that I knew this was an idealized image that few could live up to. Having been without a father for so long, any approximation—even just my father's notice— would do. Things were about to change.

More certain than gray hair and gravity, the red-and-white AARP card arrived in the mail, signaling a new chapter in my life. It was time to tackle the number-one item on my bucket list—reconnecting with my father. I finally was ready to end over four decades of fatherlessness. With me entering my fifth decade and he in his mid-70s, we were both running out of time. If anything ever was going to happen, it would be up to me.

It started simply enough. I sent my father a letter introducing myself and my life. I struggled for weeks to achieve just the right tone. Upbeat, matter-of-fact, and non-accusatory—especially that. He responded with a phone call. From there, we took turns calling each other on Sunday afternoons. Our conversations were casual and established us on a friendly footing. I sent more letters, telling him about the chaos that had been my life and how I had missed him when I was growing up. He responded by saying he had simply taken my mother's word that everything was okay when in fact, our lives constantly teetered from one brink to another. Admittedly, my mother was very good at putting on a good face for public consumption. But still, I thought, maybe unreasonably, that as a "real" father, he should have known! So as not to endanger our fragile beginning, I gave voice to my pain and anger only to my husband.

After several weeks, I planned a trip from my home in Maryland to my hometown in Kentucky to see my father. Unsure of how my mother, who still lived in the town and saw my father regularly at church, would greet this plan, I arranged to stay with my cousin for the three days I would devote to my father. The one-hour flight was the longest and most nerve-wracking of my life. I fretted over whether I had achieved enough, whether I was too overweight, whether he'd approve of my marriage, or whether I measured up to his other daughters. I desperately needed him to approve of me and like me. It was silly. I was a grown woman, yet I acted like an adolescent on a first date. In retrospect, that's exactly what it was.

I arrived at my cousin's house late Friday night and settled in to wait for my father's visit on Sunday after church. I spent Saturday shopping for clothes—I'd decided that everything I had packed was unsuitable. Sunday, when he knocked on the door, I had a moment of panic and ran to the back of the house, forcing my cousin to open the door. He walked into the house, a dapper figure carrying my face on an older male body. An instantaneous flood of love went throughout my body, and I rushed across the room to hug him. I had schooled myself to be reserved, but this embrace had been held cocked for years, only waiting for the right target. As his arms encircled me, daughterhood surged over me like an underground stream claiming light. The awkwardness I expected to feel just wasn't there. It was so profound as to be almost genetic. A call of blood to blood. I suddenly understood why adopted children search for their birth parents.

We could hardly carry on a conversation as I stared at him, looking for all the ways in which we were alike. The same facial structure. The same heavy eyebrows. The same gold-flecked brown eyes. The same laugh. We had already established in our phone conversations that we liked many of the same things, enjoyed quiet environments and times alone, and had easy-going slow-to-anger natures. But while he was content to let things unfold, I was more the type to act and make things happen. That was his excuse for not more actively connecting with me during my childhood— that he'd just been waiting for the right stimulus. I was struck by the thought that, without realizing it, I had married a man who mirrored my father in many ways.

Over the next two days, that first rush of love gave way to incessant questioning on my part. I needed to know his life. Most importantly, I needed to know why he left and why, given my close proximity, he remained removed from my life while I grew up. I already knew that the ever-changing answers I had been given by my mother were not to be trusted. I wanted the truth, and I believed my father would tell me. He did.

While explaining how he figured I did not need him, he surprised me with the story of two attempts he had made to gain custody of me. I was moved to tears. He *had* wanted me! We continued talking, and at every step, I looked for falsity and deception. Even as I confronted him with question after question, waiting for him to stumble and fail, my heart begged him not to. In some twisted way, I was daring him to stay in my life.

In my fantasy, I saw him greeting me with trumpet blasts and pomp, like a lost child, parading me around town, claiming me, and proudly presenting me to his family. Instead, it was just us two, talking and talking and then talking some more. I realized I had waited too long, and it was now too late to play the prodigal. He was too old and infirm and not really up to the task of fanfare and introducing me into his vast family. I think it all had more to do with his penchant for just letting everything stand as is rather than making things happen. I settled for being grateful for his efforts to pave the way for a relationship with his wife and daughters.

The more we talked and knew each other, the more I saw his imperfections. He did nothing to hide or excuse his placid nature (a trait that he and my husband shared). This nature contradicted my heroic fantasy dad, who would have broken down doors to rescue me and would have raged to become part of my life.

Fantasy had to give way to the reality of the man I wanted to know. I began to take note of him. His fastidiousness and the care he took about his appearance, almost to the point of dandyism. His penchant for the ease of life and aversion to conflict (again, like my husband). His outright addiction (like mine) to crossword puzzles. How much he enjoyed a good drink, a smoke, sports, or a simple television show (such as "Walker, Texas Ranger," which I learned to like). The way he talked about his daughters— now including me—was fiercely loving, yet resigned and even proud that we were our own women. His characterization of his relationship with his wife that he said had long ago become less marriage and more a comforting and constant friendship. Most puzzling was his longstanding care and affection (love?) for my mother. As I began knowing him better, it became apparent to me that although he and my mother might have been soulmates, there were no two people who didn't belong together more than they. Somehow, that insight, too, held healing of sorts.

All the while I was learning to love the real man, I was mourning the loss of the fantasy father of my childhood. After much raging and tears, I finally purged myself of the yearning that things could have been different for both of us. For me, the past was the absence of a parent I adored. For him, it was a path not taken. This was something we both sadly acknowledged, and it somehow made our bond stronger. We tacitly agreed to set aside the sadness to make room for love and our growing joy of discovery.

From that first visit, my father and I had eight years of knowing and loving each other. Despite his death nearly three years ago, I am fatherless no more.

147

# 19: Margaret: A Discordant Symphony

I have never encountered anyone like Margaret, my mother. She was capable of eliciting, simultaneously, love, anger, curiosity, and despair. Innately talented, yet highly frustrating. When I abandon the anger and blame game, I see a woman with burning ambition to achieve an upper-middle-class lifestyle and status. Yet, she remained locked in a traditional mindset that determined she could only achieve her dreams through a man—and, later me.

As a student at Tennessee State University, many fellow students worked to pay for college expenses. Margaret chose to quit when her father could no longer pay. Throughout her life, she blamed the jealousy of her siblings and their influence on her father. Before they were married, my father took a trip out of town to interview for a job. Though they had been a couple since third grade, my mother called it quits and got a new man—all without informing my father. He learned he had been replaced when he returned, went to see her, and was met by the new man. Ironically, had she followed through and married my father, she would have instantly achieved status as well as financial security. I think she regretted this her whole life. I think my father also often speculated on what could have been.

## Beginnings

Born in 1927, Margaret was the next youngest child of a patient man and a demanding mother whose loyalties lay with the fractious children from an earlier marriage. Margaret was cute and smart and grew up in a society that taught her to disdain her dark skin. She trumpeted throughout her life her place as her father's (Daddy Ernest) favorite child. It was a status to which she longed to return her whole life. Her quest to be someone's favorite often manifested itself in her use of a little-girl voice, usually directed at me. It only worked so long as I myself was a child. She found her soulmate in my father, Philip. They became a couple as third-graders and remained so through college and beyond. He was the light-complexioned son of a powerful and wealthy doctor. Her family was widely respected, comparatively darker, and mostly working-class. She bore him two daughters, then refused to leave her father's house for marriage. Spurned one time too many, my father married another woman and begat another two daughters. Still, she and Philip devotedly sat one pew behind the other each Sunday for more than sixty years.

After Philip married, Margaret chose a husband who was my father's opposite in nearly every way. He was dark, uneducated, had only initials for a name ("AB"), and made his living by gambling. She said AB represented excitement, but I think she accepted his proposal as an admission of defeat. She spent much of their marriage ridiculing him to her friends.

### *The Lost Child*

I could never understand the residual anger that always seethed around her or her refusal to fully love. After much living and therapy, I finally figured out that it couldn't be me. I'd never done a thing to the woman except exist. I thought maybe it was some self-imposed penance for letting my father get away. Maybe so, but then, I learned it was something perhaps more profound. When I was 55, my father let slip that for almost a year, I had a big sister—Virgil Anne. Margaret finally confirmed the existence of this beautiful, perfect baby of her dreams who would have loved her forever. Virgil Anne died months after her birth. In those days, grieving mothers were expected to "get over" and "get on." The grief counseling industry would not emerge for another fifty years. Even if it had existed, I don't think it would have been used by most black people, who, at that time, lived in families only recently removed from a time of forced labor when loss was frequent but work never stopped. Grief had to end once a body was in the ground.

What fear she must have felt at the news of my coming, a second child who might also arrive and leave just as she'd given her heart. Was it this fear that kept us estranged and her afraid to love fully? Did this weigh on your decision to place me first, with a wet nurse, later with a nurse to be raised, and still later with relatives? It was my cousin, Diane, with whom she resonated. Diane was so like Margaret; they could have been daughter and mother. Admittedly, Diane was an easy child to love; she was pretty, darker than I was, and happiest when getting pretty dresses.

I have to admit, when I learned about Virgil Anne, my first sympathy was for myself. I was almost not alone. It was only after Margaret's death that I began to think of her loss and how it might have changed her. Maybe she cried secretly, alone at night, before donning the expected brave-soldier face by day.

We never loved or even fought as mothers and daughters do. There was simply nothing but my bitterness and bewilderment. Later, I know she wanted it to be different. But we could not create in an instant what had never been, and so we continued in a chaotic, disjointed symphony.

### *Adagio*

A body memory from when I was two or three has comforted me throughout my life. Margaret and I often sat close, she gently and patiently guiding my child hand to print, first, my ABCs, then my name, and later, my numbers. She tirelessly read and taught me, always ready to slake my thirst for knowledge that was never quenched. Even at that young age, Margaret divined the essence of me and gave me the greatest gift—the power of the written word. Reading and the search for knowledge would forever be my muse and solace—a way to lose myself and succor my spirit.

In those early days, we were perfectly balanced. Me, beloved by Grandaddy Ernest and my nurse, Gwen. You, an inexhaustible source of knowledge and answers. I didn't want new dresses or shoes like my cousin, Diane. I was driven by another force, getting answers to the questions: What is there new to know today? What's this? How do I do that? Teach me to print my name. How do I use the sewing machine? What are these flowers called? How do I draw a kite? Dancing—first position? Piano—a first melody? In those heady first years of my life, there was never enough learning. The love of learning, the need to know, and the life of the mind, which began early, continue to define me to this day. The words "thank you" are an inadequate response to these gifts.

Our balanced world came to an end when I was abruptly sent to live with my great Aunt Carrie and Uncle Herbert, whom I had never met. During that time, my grandfather and grandmother died, and Margaret moved away with her new husband, AB. I was kept in the dark about all of it. Aunt Carrie died after eight years, and I moved in with Margaret (and AB) and started high school.

*Appassionato*—impassioned, intense

Margaret worked furiously to achieve Norman Rockwell-ness, but her efforts always fell short. For one, she just had the wrong cast—me and my stepfather—for her perfect plays. Often, her regret, despair, and anger stirred together and steeped, forming a toxic potion that endangered anyone who happened to be nearby. That "anyone" was usually me or AB. Things would start off well enough—at least enough for me to believe. But, inevitably, a small problem or two would arise, and with no warning, I would be surprised to find myself deep in that caustic brew.

*Ostinato*—unceasing, stubborn

Margaret's fantasy life was always near the surface. A prince, princess, castle, adoring subjects—was always just out of reach. Had she not held rock-solid to the belief that a man was supposed to give them to her, she could have achieved most, if not all, of her dream. Unlike most black women in our town, she had education, decent work, and options. I don't think it was laziness or the even-then old-fashioned notion of a woman's place that held her back. I think it was fear. She was afraid to try and afraid to give emotionally to another person in order to make her dreams come true. Did she think, in some minuscule corner of her mind, that her dark skin disqualified her from having the better things in life? For long periods forgot her struggles as I went off to live my life. Still, there were interludes where I played her loyal and slavering attendant. It was always short-lived. The game usually ended when she said or did something so hurtful that I had to walk away to keep from lashing out. Initially, she hated the thought of my being married ("Why did I need anyone else when I already had her?"), and she carried a grudge for the rest of her life. I have always been amazed I was such a glutton for punishment. Why didn't I do the healthiest thing and simply disappear her from my life?

She kept my attention by generating many small conflicts and crises: someone is too jealous or envious of her—her looks, her house, her clothes, her daughter. She tossed out my accomplishments as put-downs to others who were doing less well. I often hid the things that other children rushed home to crow about. Never in our lives did words of congratulation or encouragement come to me directly. When she was in her 80s, I asked her about this, and she defended her silence with the excuse that she didn't want me to get a "big head." I guess the rules were always different for me than for her.

How funny it was, her tantrum to my cousin, Diane, when my husband and I purchased our house. How could I do this with him? Why wasn't her name on the deed? She had her own house. Why begrudge me this rite of passage? It would have been funny had it not been so sad and so a testament to her despair and bereftness.

The inner strength of this small woman! Despite reality, she managed never to relinquish her vision of perfection or her sense of entitlement to a fairy princess life. She held on in spite of everything, never giving up. Surely it was hard, thankless work trying to turn a willful daughter into becoming her man. She could never step back and figure out how to turn that will and talent toward accomplishing things for herself. What energy she used trying to get others to create her fantasy life!

As an adult, I rode an emotional seesaw, bouncing between distancing myself and gushing indulgence—until the next insult hurled me back into self-imposed exile. She never seemed able to understand another person's needs or feelings. Even during the best times, Margaret maintained her anger. Anger at everything and everybody. I usually hung up the phone mid-conversation, empty and sad for us both.

*Andante*—steadily forward

While I was in college, AB gave up on Margaret and moved to his hometown of Albuquerque, New Mexico. (They would not officially divorce until decades later.) Afterwards, Diane and I shared the man title. Diane mostly took care of the emotional propping-up, and I took care of the expenses, even as I worked two jobs to pay for law school. I found it easier to pay in money rather than pain. One of her favorite games was to try and get Diane and me to compete to see which of us outshone the other in doing something for her. Diane often fell for it, and sometimes I'd play for a while, but mostly I withdrew. In later years,

Margaret would say she was afraid that if Diane and I loved each other, there would be no love left for her. I guess that was the real reason for her self-caused crises and rescues. Like a child, what she wants, she must have—immediately—and the wants never ended. More more more more. I think Diane sometimes really believed. For me, it was just another performance.

Each month (sometimes more frequently), a new crisis emerged when she felt she had been too long neglected. The crises were often comical. A visitor stole one of her precious Hummels (later found). There was a mouse in the toilet. "I'm hungry and don't want to eat any of the food that's in the house." "I think I'm having a heart attack, but I want you to come here [1,200 miles] before I go to the hospital." As I laugh, I'm sure she wished that Virgil Anne had lived. Surely, she would have been a better, more cooperative daughter.

Near the end, she repeatedly said, "You're my best and only friend." I always had to wrestle down the anger unleashed by that pleading statement. We had had no conversations that were not about her. The words I longed to hear were never said. I survived the traumas of adulthood, career, relationships, health scares—all without her. I found my own soulmate, but I still missed this thing called "family," especially as I witnessed the loving and giving relationship between Bill and his mother.

### *Denouement*

It is decades later, and the rhythmic, hypnotic electronic beep is the only sound in the darkened room. It seems to go on forever. Then, a long beep. Silence. I have done the duty of a daughter and seen Margaret into death. I leave, closing the door gently, enter the overly bright hallway and walk to the elevator. My natural irreverence cannot be repressed. It flutters to the surface in the form of a tune from "The Wizard of Oz"—*Ding Dong the Witch is Dead*. White-clad figures move around me, striding with purpose, yet I barely notice. That stupid tune follows me home. It is over at last.

### *Brio*—vigor, spirit, fire

My first breaths in a world in which Margaret is not. I inhale, and a heaviness falls away. My breath is full and deep and sweet.

# 20: Unconditional Love

"Bless her to her bonies" was Daddy Ernest's favorite saying before grabbing up my young body for hugs, kisses, and giggles. We delighted in each other. It was bliss, and it was unconditional love.

One of television's most successful and wearisome compulsive advice-giver, Dr. Phil, frequently trots out an old saw when his guests are a family with young children. To paraphrase, "Family should be the place where a child gets unconditional love. As the child goes out in the world, the family—parent, grandparent, or another person—has to be that soft place to fall." Sounds good. I think, except for a rare few, this is a lofty and unreachable goal—like satori in Buddhism.

In my life, I actually met people who had unconditional love – or at least unconditional acceptance – from their families. They had a sense of themselves and confidence that let them "be all you can be" (apologies to the Army). Their lives were by no means without conflict or difficulty, but they seemed especially resilient, able to weather bad times and bounce back. Many had siblings and extended family to rely on, so parents were not their sole source of support. I envied them. Whenever I saw them with their families, I felt my own void more acutely.

This is not the sad story it could be. I was lucky to experience acceptance once I left my hometown for college.

There, I gathered around me a group of friends – referred to in the 70s vernacular as hippies and freaks – whose boundaries of acceptance were elastic enough to accommodate my forming identity. We were anti-everything "straight," though we accepted all manner of people, including the red-neck outdoorsman. (We were against hunting but regularly and joyfully chowed down on meat.) We were a mass of contradictions in the anything-goes 70s.

In the work world, I joined another peer group, the national civil rights community. In Washington, it was run like an exclusive club with its own rules, codes of conduct, and ways of thinking. People accepted you, initially, because of your work and not for anything personal. The thought was that if you had personal issues, it meant you were neglecting or not serious about working for "the cause." I fit in superficially, but it was difficult being a black woman working in a feminist organization. The "brothers" never said it outwardly, but they considered us less-than-committed to civil rights. For them, civil rights meant black rights.

I bonded with other women of color who were trying to make it in the civil rights world. We were underdogs externally in our fight to achieve equity because the forces against us were so powerful. But, internally, we struggled for recognition and equity in our respective organizations. We had the burden (and privilege, I guess) of helping our bosses and co-workers understand we could not choose between women's rights and civil rights. Our job seemed to be to help them, in a gentle way, confront their own racism and sexism. We banded together and supported each other in any way possible. We did a scary thing and went out on our own when necessary. For example, we formed the Women of Color Access Project, which operated parallel to the feminist effort to get women appointees. We targeted women of color – wonderfully qualified but lacking a political resume. It was seen as a betrayal by many of our organizations. We made an impact. It was not much but at least it brought to the fore a number of issues, and our organizations began to evaluate their assumptions and practices.

When bipolar forced me to drop out of the Washington civil rights activist community, my network was broken. It was not intentional, I am sure, but all our contact and connection were prefaced on our work. When I was no longer involved in the day-to-day struggle, I fell by the wayside and found we had little to talk about – despite our having shared many intimate moments. My friends continued to work their crazy-making hours, and the little personal time they had was devoted to blood kin and having families. I no longer fit in their world. It was not a hard severance. We just faded from each other's lives. I can call upon many of them today and still rate a lunch date, but that is mostly because they are senior people in their organizations or retired or have children that are in or completed college. So maybe there will be a renaissance of sorts for our senior years. I am hopeful but don't depend on it.

Anyway, this is all about unconditional love and acceptance. So, I am deliriously happy to note that I have reached that lofty state with five people. For all these people, the only thing required of me is to simply be myself. The first on my list is obvious, Bill, my life mate since 1971. He just always knew who he was and was as accepting of himself as he was of others. He woke each morning full of hope about the possibilities of the day. After all these years, he is still the same.

Barbara and Elisa are friends from law school. We went to the alternative Antioch School of Law, which operated much like a law firm in which students began, from the first day, learning the actual practice of law. ASL was geared toward nontraditional students who were activists. We were a scruffy bunch, and we were combative, not giving way to the normal deference paid to law professors. Hell, our first year, we went on strike and paid tuition into an escrow account rather than to university until they met our demands. We also, along the way, made local and national laws in the areas of tenants' rights, prison reform, whistle blower, and other caselaw.

Barb was at the center of the fun. A great student, she also knew how to get people excited about joy. Wherever she was, people seemed to congregate. She found the best deals that would give us the most joy for our precious pennies. We three, Barb, Elisa, and me, just clicked. We worked together on a highly-regarded national law reporter, interned at the Congressional Clearinghouse on Women's Rights, and made any number of spontaneous trips to Appalachian cabins, New York City, the Outer Banks, and national demonstrations. She was the most enthusiastic and joyous person I knew. Elisa and I just followed along a bit lower key. In my snobbery, I attributed Elisa's reticence and quiet to her place as the eldest daughter of a Chinese immigrant family. I never knew how much that was a factor until later when I learned how she endured the ridicule and lack of nurturing that seemed to be traditionally heaped on girls. Our friendship has lasted over 40 years, and we are each other's best friends – near sisters. They have both been incredibly encouraging in every endeavor. I can count on them to "have my back," no matter what.

Jannie was an entirely different story. Our relationship was total love and caring, although sometimes I was surprised – and confused – when she disappeared into one sibling crisis or another. I didn't understand how blood kin could be more important than our relationship. In truth, it wasn't. We saw each other through breakdown and rebuilding. She was eight years older and grew up in a harsh, restrictive home responsible for mothering numerous siblings. She brought me a perspective that I sorely lacked and an anchor to the black community. Integration was not part of her life until she attended Simmons College. Circumstance seemed to conspire, and she never gained the traction one would expect. We were colleagues in the civil rights community, but that is only a small part of what she was to me. The dearest thing she did for me was to make the arduous trip from South Carolina while undergoing dialysis to see me talk through the experiences that would make up this book. My supreme regret is that I did not take what would be her last phone call. She died soon after.

My relationship with Joy came after my dropout from the civil rights community while I was servicing the bipolar disease. We met when we were both accepted into the 1989 Leadership Washington class. I applied because I needed to expand my consulting practice and sorely missed the connection to purpose-driven people. Joy headed a parent organization in Washington but had been much more for many years. I was making money hand over fist from consulting with Rockefeller Foundation and the Washington Greater Research Center. Joy was content to sit in the background. I was nervous being in the spotlight but equally afraid of being overlooked. I didn't like not being important! But, in truth, I was out of my league with this group where most of the leaders were CEOs of major corporations and nonprofits, public figures, and all, commanding more than a few resources. Still, we somehow found each other. Over the years after Leadership Washington, we have been mainstays to each other in our personal lives. I was dismayed when she decided to go to seminary, but even that steeping in religiosity did not come between us.

I possibly could have made different choices had I grown up with the foundation of unconditional love and acceptance. But, maybe, I wouldn't have liked the person I would have become. I would have missed the experience of being an "outsider" and "lesser than." Uncomfortable as it was, I would not have found my Bill, my Barb and Elisa, my Jannie, and my Joy.

# 21: Our Home

Bill and I are at the stage where we must seriously consider the move to our next and final home. I am excited, yet the move will be bittersweet. Living in one of the country's wealthiest counties has had great advantages, but the drawback is that while we will be able to sell our house at a profit, it is not enough to buy another in the area we both love. We have been on this journey to move for quite some time, but I think one of the main reasons it has taken so long is that we would both miss our home terribly.

This, our first house, was built in 1950 with typically strong bones and small closets. We bought it in 1983 and have lived here for over 30 years. When we bought it, our house was in what was considered a suburban bedroom community in which one or both adults were employed by the Federal Government. There was already one black family and one family from India. (Soon after we moved in, the Asian/Indian husband killed his wife because he found his brother visiting while he was not at home. It was a neighborhood-wide scandal for a while.) Bill and I were the only mixed-race couple. It was pretty cookie-cutter stuff.

When the Hashimis sold us the house, Mr. Hashimi spent nearly the entire time extolling his lawn. He was so proud of the work and pampering he had given to growing rich, luscious grass in front and back. He was so excited. Bill was a horticulturist, though I don't think he quite understood what that was. Among the first things Bill did was dig up all the grass and replace it with plants. We even planted a cutting of a cryptomeria, which I never thought would grow. Now, of course, when you use Google Earth, the tree shows up as the largest thing in the neighborhood.

For my part, I immediately started destroying the brightly painted rooms and carpeted inside. I worked at it every day after work and on weekends. We had very little furniture to encumber my efforts. My plan was to fix it up and sell it a couple of years later. (This was a time when the market was hot.) But, my plans did not include the expectations and joy Bill would find at seeing his plants come up. Besides that, he also installed two small ponds, complete with fish, in our tiny backyard, now depleted of grass. We had a small front and back yard and shared a wall with our neighbor, what I believe is called a semi-detached house. Another unexplained "gift" left by the Hashimis were three huge aquariums, thankfully, without fish. In the basement were one 150-gallon and two 75-gallon aquariums. These were left over from the previous owners, who also owned the local exotic fish store. It took several years to finally get rid of these assets.

I often complained our house was too small, but, in truth, it was just right for a couple with no children but with a penchant for cats. We moved in with two identical black cats, and about a year later, our friend Chuck gave us a kitten.

This kitten actually picked Bill; he became Sidney, and he would totally change both our lives. Bill always rushed home directly from work so he could see Sidney. And it seemed Sidney, in turn, was anxiously awaiting Bill's arrival. When Bill walked in the door, Sidney often tripped over his large feet in a rush to get to Bill. As Sidney grew larger, he jumped from the floor directly into Bill's arms. Eventually, he became a traveling buddy when Bill drove to and from Kentucky to see his mother. Most people exclaimed they had never seen a cat as gentle as Sidney. He was large, fluffy, and sported auburn-colored fur that included a full ruff. His appearance got us interested in Maine Coon cats, which he most resembled. We bought him a female companion (by this time, our original two cats had died), and they had kittens which were immediately snapped up by our friends. Needless to say, we went overboard with buying and birthing Maine Coon cats until once we had 19 kittens (we thought a cat couldn't get pregnant while nursing)!

About two or three years after purchase, our house played sanctuary to my bipolar disorder. That was when I was trying to figure out my "problem" and when I was on a changing cycle of medications. The lows were easy to handle: I kept appointments that I had to, slept in too much, and did a lot of at-home work. I maintained. Still, the disease was, in my mind, too much to cope with and keep the dream job I loved. Manic episodes, on the other hand, required I enlist my house as an accomplice. Mania sent me to repaint the walls (including a grey and silver bathroom) and nail all the living room furniture on the wall. Bill was normally tolerant—except once. At home alone one day, I determined I needed a beach experience, so I set to create one in my living room. I spread out a large shower curtain, placed and partially filled a child's inflatable wading pool, and made a beach-appropriate drink. Bill came home just as I was prepared to scatter one of three bags of sand. Gentle reason ended my beach fantasy. To this day, Bill blames this adventure for the seemingly unremovable spots on the ceiling of his basement office/studio.

During our 30 plus years of occupancy, the neighborhood transformed to more than 90 percent Latino— along with us, the original African American family, and one new African family. It is still a bedroom community, though adults leave each day for different kinds of jobs. Bill, being the outgoing one of us, has integrated us into a whole posse of friends who speak varying amounts of English and who call him "Mister Bill." We have become comfortable using pantomime and uttering broken, mispronounced Spanish words. In summer, we sit outside, listen to backyard celebrations, and look with pleasure at the shirtless young men dancing to Latin music. Our spoils are heaping plates of homemade pupusas and tamales.

Just as houses settle, we too have settled into a comfortable existence giving the house a little nudge here and there and creating wonderful garden greenspace. Our house can lay claim to a few peculiarities that make her unique. Fruits and melons set on the table ripen so fast that the process should be the subject of a scientific inquiry. All but the newest windows and doors are off-kilter. Anyone using Bill's basement bathroom must be under 5 feet 5 inches or slump over a lot. Bill is 5 feet 11 inches. The bones are good and sturdy, if not modern. The steps are good and solid, but for the two, they creak loudly when you step on them. I fondly think of it as our own intruder warning system.

Even as we become increasingly aware that this is not a home to age-in-place, we still cling to it. Since we could never afford a more suitable house in our wealthy county, I am resolved and sometimes even looking forward to our move to Kentucky. I have done my part to say "yes" to the move. I leave the actual date to Bill. (It used to be the other way around.) When we said we would move, I immediately began purging closets and packing things. I should have taken a cue from Bill—he packed nothing. On the contrary, he entered into a fury fixing the house with new windows, flooring, bathroom upgrade, etc.

Moving forward, the house has played host to our "second" careers. When we cleaned out the basement, Bill moved in a large easel and began painting in earnest. After a successful first solo exhibit, prizes, and recognition, I have heard only distant references to moving. In the meantime, I won a slot in a prestigious writing retreat in California which re-energized my fantasy of becoming a writer. In fact, when I returned from the Mesa Refuge writing fellowship, I found Bill had built me a small, screened-in porch for writing—my own personal writing shed. This is where we each enjoy special garden "rooms" throughout the year. It's where Bill gets to experiment with an area devoted to night-blooming plants. It is where something has finally bloomed after years of anticipation. It is where we remained safe during COVID in 2020. As we must leave, despite protests from our neighbors and friends, we anticipate a deep loss, like saying goodbye to an old, comforting friend.

# 22: Rich

Based purely on economics, I grew up poor, lived comfortably, and was firmly rooted in the middle and upper-middle-class lifestyle. I had access to things like private dance, piano, elocution lessons, camps and summer trips, school programs and activities that required fees, etc. Poor people in Hopkinsville lived in public housing and received commodities and free lunches. None of these applied to me. Then, there were the "dirt poor," which described my husband's life as a child in which he felt pressured early to get a paying job and contribute to the support of the household. Sometimes they were short of food. The focus of my life was school and learning, excelling, and becoming somebody. A weekly allowance also distinguished me from those in more dire straits. In Hopkinsville, the designations were fairly fluid. You could move from dirt poor, to poor, to even comfortable—all dependent on a job and luck. Comfortable mostly included teachers, those employed by the state in janitorial, clerical, the post office, and other steady work where salaries were set by state or federal authority—though you did have to get recommended by the local politicos.

If you were poor and wanted something more in life, you had to radically excel in school to gain the attention and help of teachers and counselors. By the time I moved to seventh grade I was put in the college track along with the children of doctors, lawyers, and such. In middle school, there were very few black students; all the rest of the black students went to classes other than mine. The black high school closed as I entered ninth grade. I remained with my track, which added only three additional black students. By graduation, I had spent six years looking sat at the back of Helen Grayson's head.

Counselors paid little attention to black students at that time. Most were counseled to consider community college or trade school. This happened to me though I was in the college-bound group. When my counselor learned my mother and father were college-educated and that my grandfather was a doctor, she changed her tune and started showing me college brochures. Other black students who went on to college had someone at home who advocated for them. I had nothing but my own desperate will to leave Hopkinsville. I think skin color also played a role in the counselors' change of mind. Being light-skinned, I must have been smart and destined for more than a factory job.

We had some kids who were "dirt" poor. These kids often went without meals, took on part-time jobs, and often had to find temporary shelter to escape their home environment. Their home did not include a reverence for learning, reading, or other such things; the center of their home life was survival. They sometimes smelled because of a lack of hygiene facilities or clean clothes. I often invited them for dinner and sometimes bought them books, shirts, and other items. They were ostracized, but many found the inner strength to continue their work and graduate from high school. These are some of the successes I most admire.

It was my early l life in Hopkinsville that made me into a philanthropist. As a child, I paid for the errant treat, a movie ticket, or a book. The tradition continues to this day. I have no foundation bearing my name. I am not a one-percenter or even a 50-percenter. I live an economically depressed lifestyle that belies my education—no big house, no golden zip code (though I guess Montgomery County, Maryland is zip enough), no executive or partner parachute. My neighborhood has become Latino Central in Montgomery County. Montgomery County is one of the nation's wealthiest; I live in the blue-collar anomaly.

I remember as a child, my friend Gloria, a year younger than me. She was absolutely brilliant. She had several siblings (all sisters and one brother), an authoritarian father married to a much-younger wife. Gloria was the odd child: bookish, physically frail, thinking her own thoughts. Her parents just thought her odd and did not support her bookish nature. I remember buying several books for her. It did not make us close friends. Sometimes I wanted that but quickly evolved to seeing my contribution to genius. She went on to do great things and become known internationally. We came together in our later years, and it was wonderful. No gratitude expected, just connection and an acknowledgment of a shared past. There were others, such as the kids who could not afford the fried bologna sandwiches we all bought for a nickel on the way home from school. I always had money, so I could host others. I liked it handled quietly. No reward. I liked having a secret with another person.

I think those experiences honed my thoughts. You don't give to get something back. But, still, the payback for me was a sense of pleasantness and fulfillment. This pattern carried over to my young adult years and even today. I can't stand that someone I know has needs that are not met. I've stepped into the breach many, many times with no thought of recompense. I think that's the way it should be: if you have and someone needs, then the way is clear that you should give. I still maintain this basic philosophy, but it has grown up over the years.

I classify my philanthropy into three types: altruistic, mindless, and self-protective. The first, altruistic is based on personal relationships. Someone I know has a need, and I try my best to fulfill it. The need could be money, or it could be something more active. A simple act was when my friend, Joy, was caring for an ailing mother and needed to provide her with more food. For several weeks, Bill and I shopped at Costco and bought additional items to deliver to Joy. That was a rather simple example of giving. Another more long-term act was when Bill and I helped a young man who previously had no prospects enter and complete nursing school. Of course, I had to help him overcome his macho perspective about nurses. Now he is a registered nurse, working full-time and getting ready to buy a home. Another young man got a chance to attend college far away from the drug court in which he was born. Buying books and a winter coat were a small price to pay for his success.

A couple of Latino friends share their difficulty in making ends meet. Bill generates horticulture jobs that he works with them (despite the physical toll it takes on him and the time away from painting). That's just the way it goes. People need, and you respond. I would love to say no, but it doesn't seem we are made that way.

Other altruistic giving did little to better the lives of giftees. My close friend, and partner in depression, could always identify a specific thing she needed to get "set to right" again. I would obediently trot along and provide it: clothes, shoes, computer, filing cabinet, etc. A quiet thank you would be forthcoming. I waited and waited for these things to help her turn around, but they never did. It would have been better for her to deal with her depression. It made me understand why foundations required each request to be in the form of a well-thought-out proposal that demonstrated some insight and identified outcomes. I did learn from that experience and now, just listen to the woes and needs expressed by some of my friends while offering nothing. I even started turning down requests to provide free legal services. Actually, I started resenting these requests.

I name my other type of philanthropy as mindless giving. That usually comes in the form of purchasing a ticket or donating to a cause or organization. Depending on how passionate I feel, the donation may result in more engagement, such as volunteering, attending a march, or other events. Usually—no, always, this gets you on the list for a future appeal. After a while, some may drop off the giving list while others may be added.

The third type of philanthropy has the purpose of self-protection. This is in the vein of "it's easier to give than to engage." This was the relationship with Margaret, my mother. Margaret treated me and others as her personal ATMs. "Give me" and "I need" were constants in her speech. My altruism turned off cold at that. There was no reciprocity to the relationship since she never gave (not even a birthday card).

For her, a good relationship was when she was being given lots of attention, always accompanied by something of monetary value. In her later years, when she expected closeness, it was not there; neither of us knew how to give it. It still saddens me that we never made it as a family.

This philosophy even emerges in my marriage. We don't eat the last because we subconsciously save the last for the other person. A lot of stuff gets wasted that way. When I just mention wanting something in passing, the next thing I know, Bill has bought it. Sometimes he keeps buying it beyond my point of desire. He tells me of growing up, and all food on the table was up for grabs. No one asked about taking the last thing. I have met several of his friends who seem to think they have to grab all the food or there will be no more. It bothers me.

I wonder, sometimes, whether my status sense as being mostly comfortable rather than needy is the basis for my philanthropy. There were only a couple of times food was scarce, and that was due to the foolishness of my mother. Still, I never went hungry. I never had desperate want.

I asked several people of diverse means to classify themselves as poor, comfortable, rich, or wealthy based on their own definitions of the terms. I knew all these people and their economic situations. Only one person identified as poor. Her reason for economic poverty lay in other areas. Everyone else, including the three one-percenters, classified themselves as comfortable. One person, who had her own private jet, repeatedly assured me it was only a "small" jet. There was an overall discomfort in claiming rich or wealthy like both terms carried shame. Admittedly, my group consisted of those who could be considered "liberal." All knew that I had intimate knowledge of their economic status. Some on the rich-to-wealthy continuum tried to deflect and talk about things other than money, like being rich in friendships or wealthy in spirituality. One person gave me her definitions of the categories that resonated with me.

---

I am **Comfortable** because my time is my own. I am finished with 20 years of formal schooling. I am finished with 35-40 years of traditional office work. I am thankful for social security and retirement funds, even though they are based on my contributions. I qualify for reduced property taxes, a property credit and water bill credit. I could almost laugh. I am not required to take continuing legal education courses anymore or pay the attorney registration fee. The educational requirements, financial obligations, daily grind, professional qualifications, employee evaluations are gone or are minimal.

---

**Poor** means having a need to compare oneself to other people. A person believes she has less and is therefore worth less. It is accepting that things and goals are meant for others only.

**Rich** means being open to all possibilities and accepting some of them. It is being able to see an invisible welcome sign leading to a person, place or thing.

**Wealthy** means having lots of cash and things that can be converted into cash like real estate and investments. It is using cash to make more cash without having to go to work. It is having more cash than anyone would ever need to spend.

---

I like my self-defined status of being comfortable because it provides the most flexibility. As one who is comfortable, I can connect with people from poor to wealthy without qualms. If I were rich or wealthy, I think I would have to fend off the public and possibly have staff to protect my distance from people and life experience. At one time in my life, I was what one could call rich, but bouts of mania associated with bipolar disorder took care of that. There are regrets, but not many.

Anyway, where do I end up with all this perambulating? I guess there are a couple of conclusions. First, if it feels good to give, then do it. Second, absolve yourself of any responsibility for the gift. Third, expect to be disappointed.

# 23: Living in Prime Time

In his book, *Prime Time Health*, Dr. William Sears defines prime time as age 50 or older. Of course, his book is focused on healthy aging. He says prime timers are, health-wise, in repair mode.

So, I am in prime time. I expected many of the physical changes, although I admit being surprised when my husband started making involuntary grunting sounds when he sat or rose. When brought to his attention, his inevitable response is always "What noise?".

I have been thinking more and more about the preciousness of prime time. As is my wont, I posed a question to friends:

*Can you name two things that surprised you about living in prime time. Your surprises can be not so great or they can be delightful.*

Some of the more interesting responses included:

*Delight at being able to step out of the mainstream. I kinda like slower.*

*Finding joy in the little things.*

*My mind always thinks I'm younger until I move my body.*

*Preciousness of time.*

*How quickly the AARP card came.*

*Cherishing alone time.*

*Enjoying grandchildren and discounts.*

*Becoming compassionate.*

*I haven't slowed down enough to think about it.*

*Having a reality that is not always respected by young people.*

*Learning to respect that people, especially young people, are operating from their own reality and experience.*

*I care less about what people think—they can just accept you or hear you at your 100 proof.*

These were all informative, but my surprises were a little different. The first surprise has been finding myself frequently chastising the mirror and accusing it of lying. I guess I suffer from that boomer disease that went by several slogans: "forever young," "trust no one over 30," and "the Youth Movement." As a consequence, I regularly rail at and berate the mirror, "What's that old face doing on my 30-year-old self?" I guess it's hard to totally recover from youthful arrogance. At least I have learned to laugh at myself. Just as boomers challenged, redefined, and rewrote social rules and institutions, I am happy we are rewriting "old age." I guess some young folks feel they are never going to get shut of us!

The second surprise is I have found my way to a truer, more real, more authentic life. I live closer to the core, so to speak. Though I still indulge at times in pettiness, this blanket of contentment seems to have enfolded me. It just arrived through no effort of my own. Make no mistake; I still have ambition enough for two; and, perhaps foolishly, plans for future achievement. I know I have fewer years ahead than I have behind me, but it hasn't stopped me from dreaming about "making my mark." I don't look too closely at defining what that is; I'll know it when it happens.

My prime time has been an exhilarating time of growth and creativity. The body has been failing—mostly because I am too lazy to stick with a program. But, my mind! It surges! Bill and I have both found prime-time careers – him as an artist and me as a writer. We always wanted these careers but were too practical to act on our dreams. We are fortunate to have reconnected to our passions with time and health to indulge them. Sometimes, as Bill and I enjoy afternoon tea, we shake our heads and say, "what took us so long?". Bill was an art student when we first met but gave up pursuing a career as an artist to support me while I went to law school. After the bipolar hit and my prospects for a law career dimmed, he continued to maintain a steady job to help support us. He loved his years as a horticulturist and brought an artist's eye and sensitivity to everything he did. Now, with his retirement, I take as much joy with him finally getting to paint as I do with me seriously pursuing writing. I have always written, for work or privately, but now, somehow, I want to communicate my thoughts and feelings to the world. That is entirely new.

Like a lot of boomers, we neglected our savings, and so we live on a shoestring, but we've found we don't really need much. We afford what we need and often enjoy indulgences. Our one "gap" is family. We have cats whom we love dearly, but no children and only a few estranged relatives. My cousin, Diane, died and ended my almost-sister bond. Bill outlived his parents and both brothers. When Margaret died, that ended my last familial obligation. My friends talk of grandchildren and family vacations, and other gatherings. A group of people who are each others' "given," a connectedness of blood I have never known except with Bill. I have a few close friends, but they have families that come first. I would like to "come first" to a group of people. To me, that would be the warmth of family. Sometimes I yearn for that though I am mostly thankful to escape some of the drama.

# 24: Right of Return

The "right of return," codified in national and international law as well as in religion, propounds the inalienability of a person's right to something called "home." Maybe it is even hard-wired into the DNA of all beings. For some, home is sited in the heart and mind; for others, it is tied to a physical place, like Jews' relationship with Israel. I spent decades searching, finding, losing, and finding again my home in my work, Bill, and my circle of women friends. Now, finally, everything has converged, and I can say home is a place that lives within me. It will soon also include a special place back in Kentucky since Bill, and I have decided to spend the rest of our lives in the state of our birth.

I have held at bay, for over thirty years, my husband's desire to return to Kentucky. Each time the subject came up, a feeling of sickness overcame me as I remembered the hostility that I suffered at the hands of racists while growing up in the commonwealth. And so, I'd make yet another excuse, and we would continue on. Even if I wanted to reclaim my birthright, my state did not want to claim me. That was my thinking. My mind conjured up scenarios in which Bill and I were harassed and even attacked by white people who couldn't stand to see a white man married to a black woman. I had real fear—and it was not unfounded. Even now, the Southern Law Poverty Center has identified more than twenty-five alt-right hate and white-nationalist groups operating in the state, even nearby Lexington. Interestingly, once the decision to move had been made, it was Bill who asked if I wanted to remain in the Washington area so I could help fight Trump. He knew me so well. [I had thoughts about writing a chapter about Bill, but the more I thought about it, I found I couldn't. To write about Bill is like writing that I breathe air. He is that much a part of me. Besides, he would hate the idea.]

I have seething anger at injustice and the restrictions imposed by race and gender. I have hated the idea that my white friends could so freely move and locate nearly anywhere in this country that is my own, while I, on the other hand, no less patriotic, had to add "potential for violence" as one of the criteria for finding my place. Still, I wanted Bill to have his dream. And, in truth, I have grown weary of Washington and the heaviness of being so close to the Trump orbit and all that he represents. Bill and I looked at likely places and finally found one. So, we will make our home in Berea—a town founded by abolitionists and home to Berea University, which gave kids of coal miners their first opportunities for higher education. Berea will be our little island in an often-hostile state.

And so, I am again reinventing myself.

As I am closing one chapter of my life, and another is opening. My latest "reinvention" integrates four identities.

Writer. Practitioner of faith. Dynamic Living Warrior. Striver for an America that values all its people and is willing to take a hard look at itself. These identities pretty well represent the sum total of my life, but it has taken more than seven decades for me to claim them all.

I have always wanted to be a writer. Over my career, I have authored scores of boring technical and persuasive documents, but these did not call for the vulnerability or freedom of creativity I desired but was afraid to pursue. I have been too insecure about calling myself a writer. But no more. I don't know if I'm good at it or whether anyone cares to read what I write. The bottom line is that I want to give free rein to the writer in me. Good, mediocre, or bad, I want to find forums in which to articulate what I see, feel, believe, and imagine.

The second leg is spirituality and faith. I have always been a spiritual person but no particular religion and have made a lifelong study of many. I have a soft spot for the tenets of all religions. I just can't bring myself to reject any whole cloth. But my personal journey is the renewed practice of my own hodge-podge of Buddhism with a friendly nod and handshake of christianity. I like the faiths and philosophies that are founded in the belief that we can become buddhas in our lifetimes and that give lay practitioners a role as important as priests. I like those faiths that call for believers to keep an open and challenging mind that holds leaders accountable. Few meet all my expectations, thus the cobbled-together of my own unique set of beliefs.

The third aspect of my new self deals with health—mental and physical. I have talked previously about my mental health challenges. The drugs I needed to cope with them resulted, over the years, in weight gain, which in turn led to high blood pressure, diabetes, and a host of other maladies. Finally, I am turning that around, and in doing so have found a new passion. Like an evangelist, I want everyone I know (and don't know) to embrace self-love and to show it by becoming the healthiest, most dynamic, happiest old crones they can be. I wish this for young people as well, but it is my peers to whom I can best speak. Especially women of color. I know first-hand how women my age, black women, in particular, have sacrificed self-care for the so-called "greater good," be it children and family, career, social betterment, whatever.

Fourth, I remain one who believes in the rhetoric of America (even after the horror of January 6 and the cowardice of our leaders) and will continue my fight to make sure that reality lives up to the dream.

When I talked about all this with my friend TaRessa and told her of my impending move back to the land of my birth, she said that I wasn't becoming retired; I was becoming "re-fired." I'm counting on that.

*Thank you, Dear Reader, for taking the journey with me in this first writing effort. I hope you have had fun. See you in the next book.*

*VG Brooks*

# 25: An Addendum: Worries

I am, by nature, a worrier. This started in my childhood. With every opportunity or wonderful thing, I held worry in the back of my mind. I think this tendency was cemented by childhood days preparing for nuclear war. Despite relatively good luck in the face of poor decisions, I maintained my Cassandra persona—hidden, yet powerfully there.

I admit I worried when Trump got elected and for each and every day of his term. I worried that hate became acceptable and even codified. The worries have increased and I now continue to worry about:

- Trump's influence and the total wackiness of the Republican Party (I can cast aspersions; I used to be one.);

- The inability of American leaders and common folk to engage in reasoned, polite discourse;

- The violence that is so close to the surface that it explodes at the least conflict;

- COVID 19—once labelled by Millennials as the "boomer doomer." (Well, that tide has turned, hasn't it.);

- American stubbornness that refuses to use available vaccines to help us defeat COVID;

- Anti-Asian hate and violence;

- Death of black people at police hands;

189

- Rollback to Jim Crow voting rules;

- The devaluing dollar that means very lean years for seniors;

- The age of misinformation;

- Foreign cyber attacks and interference with US elections—and those in the US who seem to glory in this;

- Afghan women, left to suffer under reinstatement of anti-women laws and rules;

- A President (Biden) who is kind but lacks dynamism;

- A Kamala Harris who may not be ready to run in 2024; and, a Donald Trump who will run whether he is fit or not;

- The Delta variant and what others could be around the corner;

- The large number of people who get all their news from sensationalist media;

- Getting old and not having accomplished all my goals;

- A major chronic illness;

- Outliving my dearest Bill.

The list could go on forever. All I need do is tune into CNN, public radio, or even the alarmist news media. I can take solace that so many are in my same expanding boat.

Some worries and fears will not occur in my lifetime; I am both relieved and saddened. Relieved I will not have to endure, but saddened not to be able to witness. I am hopeful that young people will at last take up the reins and kick us old farts out of power.

V.G. Brooks resides in suburban Maryland, less that 30 miles from the nation's capitol. She lives with her life partner and their two Maine Coon cats.

Milton Keynes UK
Ingram Content Group UK Ltd.
UKHW022244040823
426363UK00009B/107